Our Homes on Indigenous Lands

Our Homes on Indigenous Lands:
Stories of My Ancestors Across Turtle Island

Mali Bain

Copyright © 2022 Mali Bain

Cataloguing data available from Library and Archives Canada
978-0-88839-741-6 [paperback]
978-0-88839-748-5 [epub]

All rights reserved. No part of this publication may be reproduced, stored in a retrieval system or transmitted, in any form or by any means, electronic, mechanical, audio, photocopying, recording, or otherwise (except for copying permitted by Sections 107 and 108 of the U.S. Copyright Law and except for book reviews for the public press), without the prior written permission of Hancock House Publishers. Permissions and licensing contribute to the book industry by helping to support writers and publishers through the purchase of authorized editions and excerpts. Please visit www.accesscopyright.ca.

Illustrations and photographs are copyrighted by the author or the Publisher unless stated otherwise.

Cover Design: J. Rade
Production & Design: J. Rade, M. Lamont
Editor: D. Martens

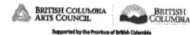

We acknowledge the support of the Government of Canada through the Canada Book Fund and the Canada Council for the Arts, and of the Province of British Columbia through the British Columbia Arts Council and the Book Publishing Tax Credit.

Hancock House gratefully acknowledges the Halkomelem Speaking Peoples whose unceded, shared and asserted traditional territories our offices reside upon.

Published simultaneously in Canada and the United States by

HANCOCK HOUSE PUBLISHERS LTD.

19313 Zero Avenue, Surrey, B.C. Canada V3Z 9R9
#104-4550 Birch Bay-Lynden Rd, Blaine, WA, U.S.A. 98230-9436
(800) 938-1114   Fax (800) 983-2262
www.hancockhouse.com   info@hancockhouse.com

Table of Contents

Acknowledgements 3
Dedication 5
Prologue: Kenya, Another British Settler Colony 7
Introduction: Answering a Canadian Question 11
Background: A Place-Based Family History 15

Part 1. Journeys to One Small Private Island 19
1. Unceded Territories: And the Place Called
   Jedediah Island 21
2. One Small "Private" Island, 1890–1910s 35
3. Ouentironk (Lake Simcoe): And Treaties 45
4. East End London to Ouentironk (Lake Simcoe), 1870s . 51
5. Portage la Prairie 59
6. Harry and Mary Ann: Ouentironk to Métis Land, 1880s 63
7. The Jelly Connection: Jellyby, Ontario, 1800s 67

Part 2. Way Back: 1640–1800s 73
8. Epekwitk (PEI): Its Original Inhabitants 75
9. "The First Bain": William Bain of Epekwitk,
   1760s–1890s 83
10. Francis Bain and the Fossil Fern of Epekwitk,
    1842–1894 89
11. Wabanaki Confederacy and Pemaquid 97
12. New England Settlers, 1635–1740s 103
13. Lenape and Susquehannock of the Delaware River . . 107
14. 'We Ye Ancient Swedes': Peter Rambo and
    Brita Mattsdotter, 1640–1680s 111

15. Strathroy's "First Settler," Daniel Springer, 1780s 119
16. 61+ Crossings: "It's complicated" 123

Part 3. Arrivals on Coast Salish Territory, 1890–1920s . . . 127
17. Coast Salish territory and Snauq 129
18. A Flood of Settlers .135
19. Bain Aunts in Kerrisdale: Mabel and Nell, 1910s–1920s 139
20. Will Bain: From War to Treaty 5, 1915–1920s 145
21. Letters from Vancouver in the 1920s 153
22. Stó:lō territory: Fort Langley, 1920s 161
23. Mt. Pleasant, 1910s 167
24. A Sojourn Down Under, 1908 173
25. 1909: Winnie and Morris of Mt. Pleasant 179
26. Jedediah Tragedies: Life and Death in the 1910s 185
27. The Ancestor I Hope to Be – and an Invitation 191

Epilogue: The Families 193
Related Reading 195

Acknowledgements

My world turned upside down when, in an elective course during my master's, Dr. Dory Nason assigned the book Decolonizing Methodologies, written by Māori author Linda Tuhiwai Smith. Tuhiwai Smith describes the "imperial gaze" with which white colonial researchers, settlers, and travellers describe the places they visit, and the people they encounter there. As I read her words, something finally sank in: colonization isn't just about what happens in other countries. As a Canadian, I am not a neutral third party. I live in a British and French settler-colony. To paraphrase Mi'kmaq researcher Marie Battiste, I am inextricably marinated in colonialism.

It's one thing to name this fact and another to know what to do with the realization. Dr. Coll Thrush loaned me his copy of Victoria Freeman's Distant Relations: How My Ancestors Colonized North America. Her thoughtful work inspired me to ask questions about the way my own family is connected to place, history, and colonization.

What you see now would never have begun, let alone been published, without the mentors, colleagues, and professors at the University of British Columbia whose pointed questions led to this project. Marie Battiste and Sákéj, Michael Marker, Tracy Friedel and my master's supervisor Shauna Butterwick taught me to question my assumptions. Norma Commodore of Xyólheméylh helped me realise how little I really know about Indigenous-settler relationships.

This work very nearly did not happen—for fear of not doing it right, for fear of saying the wrong thing, for fear of embarrassment years from now when I have learned so much more. I am grateful to friends, relatives, and others who helped and encouraged me to continue this project, in particular David Bain, Grayson Bain, Trevor Bain, Sarah Gullins, Robyn Heaslip, and Eileen Bentley. I'm also so thankful to the keen eye and insightful comments provided by David Giesbrecht, Shauna Butterwick, Autumn Knowlton, Kerry Davie, and Diane Bain. Thank you to Myles and the team at Hancock House Publishing, for believing in this book.

Finally, thank you to the Skwx̱wú7mesh (Squamish), Selílwitulh (Tsleil-Waututh), and xwməθkʷəy̓əm (Musqueam) nations, on whose lands I wrote and edited this book.

Dedication

This work is dedicated to the memory of Elizabeth Henry.

As part of the research leading to her master's thesis, she led learning circles inviting participants to explore place-based histories within one neighbourhood in the city of Vancouver. The process she led was personal, complicated, partial, and honest; I aspire to no less in my work.

Prologue: Kenya, Another British Settler Colony

This story begins on the other side of the world, over a long cup of tea. I was volunteering as a teacher in Maai Mahiu, Kenya, and had made the trek to visit a local settler couple, the Mayers.

"Here's a photo of the Rift Valley as it was." John Mayer leaned back to look at a black-and-white photo framed in wood, just above the window. He was in his sixties or so, with an accent more British than anything else and a penchant for telling stories.

He and his wife lived in a solid stone bungalow with dark wooden furniture, welcoming guests with fire-warmed tea and handmade shortbread. John told tales of travel by plane in the 1950s, when he was a boy travelling to boarding school in England. It was a three-day journey in total: first a flight from Kenya to the Suez, then over the Mediterranean to Spain, then one last leg to England.

We were seated at a long, wooden table with a view down a long, sloping lawn, with huge, spreading acacia trees and deep, dried ruts in the road down the hill. To the left, where I had walked up the stone steps, a noisy spring rippled and sucked at the roots of the acacias. Beyond the thorny branches, the misty expanse of the Escarpment and the Rift Valley of central Kenya: deforested almost completely, a place where dust blew into your eyes and never got out.

"This was the land given to my father—over 200,000 hectares. Look at the landscape—what do you see? It was all green back then, covered in trees..."

I sat in a cracked-leather chair at the Mayers' and looked at the milk swirling in my mug of Kenyan tea. I eyed the dried steer horns on the mantel, the rust-red crust of dirt splashed up against the house, and the thick-framed wall photos.

It was hard to believe that John's father had himself owned hundreds of thousands of hectares of land—this entire vista, everything visible from the Mayers' house. The area is still called kwa-Mayer by some people—literally, the "place of the Mayers." The land had not been purchased in any normal meaning of the word; it was "acquired" by the British Crown, then granted to British subjects by right of the British Crown.

"We let the rest of the land go back after Independence, back to the government."

Something about that way of speaking—"we let the land go back"—caught my ear and my heart. The phrase implied generosity, a sense of moral high ground. What does it look like to "let land go back"? What land gets "given back," and what doesn't, and why? Why is the Mayers' land so green, verdant, literally flowing with spring water, while residents of nearby Maai Mahiu lay out thin white pipes to collect trickles of water from far-off muddy streams?

I wondered if the "white Kenyans" feel comfortable with their lives—living in verdant green springs on the edge of desert, going to their country clubs for tea, driving their white Land Rovers to air-conditioned coffee shops. I couldn't help but think that white

Kenyans—the Mayers, for example—were not "real" Kenyans; they were merely British settlers in Kenya. Their accents were British, not Kenyan; many became wealthy on Kenyan land.

But then again, what makes a real Kenyan? Is it the skin or the birth certificate or familiarity with the smell of roasting corn—Or something much less tangible?

I left their home that afternoon and journeyed back to the town of Maai Mahiu, the rest of kwa-Mayer. As my months in Kenya ended, and throughout the long journey home to Canada, fragmented thoughts emerged:

> *If they're not "real" Kenyans, then am I a "real" Canadian?*
>
> *What does it mean that my parents, even my grandparents, were born in Canada—whose land were they on?*
>
> *We didn't ask to be born here, and besides, it's not like we had lots of land...*
>
> *What is there to "give back," and whose is it, anyway?*

What I saw in white Kenyans was in many ways a mirror of my own existence. Canada and Kenya have so many similarities. Both are British settler colonies; it's just that one happens to be more than 90 percent of local origin; the other, more than 90 percent immigrants.

It was so easy for me to judge the Mayers and yet so hard for me to see my own context in this place we call Canada: a British and French settler colony. As I returned from Kenya, I began to ask questions about my ancestors' and my own connection to the lands we currently live, love, and play on.

Introduction:
Answering a Canadian Question

Back in Canada, I was on Gambier Island sitting with a circle of women. One participant asked another, "What is your ethnic origin?" A variation on the "Where are you from?" question that people of colour have faced on Turtle Island (North America) for hundreds of years.

One by one, we answered: the first woman to speak was of Mayan ancestry, another Taiwanese, another Kenyan. And as people began to answer around the room, it became clear who hadn't yet answered: the white folks, the people who did not see themselves as "ethnic." Slowly, each of us took our turn: "English/Irish," "a mix of things," "English/Scottish/German." In contrast to our confident "ethnic" counterparts, our responses seemed a bit stilted, self-conscious, uncertain. The last woman to respond said "I don't know"; apart from where her parents were born, she didn't know anything about her family's origins.

I've been asked this question all my life: "Where are your ancestors from, originally?" and up until recently my answer has generally been vague, canned: either "English, Scottish, Irish," "English,Scottish, German," or "European mongrel," just to be safe.

Years ago I attended a workshop where, as participants, we stood on a map of Canada. The facilitator, an Indigenous woman, asked us to stand where we were born; then where our parents were born; then our grandparents. By the time she got to our great-grandparents, the room had cleared to the edges of the map. But she was still standing there, in Treaty 6 territory, where her people had been since time immemorial. In each of the places my ancestors have lived, Indigenous peoples can go back two, five, 15 generations and bring back a simple answer: since time immemorial, we have been in and of this place.[1]

I feel a sense of responsibility to know my own people, to know where I come from, and perhaps from that journey, I will have a better sense of what I bring with me—consciously and unconsciously. I'm sharing a set of responses, stories, and thoughts on the question: Where have my ancestors lived? I'm looking for a better understanding of the context of the places they came to call home.

I expected to locate about five generations of settlers, with origin stories going back to PEI (and maybe Ontario), then back to Europe. Instead, I ended up going back over 350 years, with origins in Sweden, Ireland, and Germany, and with more questions and uncertainties than I started with. I've chosen to focus on my ancestors' histories in "North America," rather than following them back to the lands they sailed from; that will need to be another project.

But first—what about this term, North America? I've always wondered. When I looked it up, I learned that America is actually an Anglicized version of the name of Amerigo Vespucci, an Italian explorer who mapped some of the eastern coast of South America for Europeans.

---

[1] "Since time immemorial" are the words used in the Stó:lō Historical Atlas. Stó:lō Heritage Trust. (2001). A Stó:lō-Coast Salish Historical Atlas. (K. T. Carlson, Ed.). (Vancouver: Douglas & McIntyre, 2001).

In other words, the name of this entire continent is based on that of an Italian explorer who never once set foot in the lands we now call North America.

There's another word for this chunk of land that Europeans started referring to as "North America": Turtle Island. The name comes from an Anishinaabe/Ojibwe creation story, in which the land of the Anishinaabe was created from the back of a large turtle after a great flood.[2] This is a story from only one of the hundreds of nations whose territories cover these lands, but at least it's not from Italy.

This book begins and ends on the western edge of Turtle Island, where I currently live and where the branches of my family converge. On the Bain (paternal) side of my family, I trace back the Bain line as well as maternal lines of my grandmother (Barker) and great-great-grandmother (Dockendorff). On the Jelly (maternal) side, I trace back the Jelly line as well as maternal lines of my great-grandmother (Foote) and great-great-grandmother (Brooks). In all cases, I continued to trace my family lineage back to the point where I found a birthplace somewhere off Turtle Island. I start and end the narrative with the Jelly/Foote families and their residence on a small island off the coast of BC, Jedediah Island.

Part 1 begins on Jedediah Island, and then traces back to the places where the Foote and Jelly families settled in the years before Jedediah. Part 2 explores a broader network of ancestors from the Bain side of the family, exploring stories of settlement and colonization as far back as the 1600s on the eastern edge of Turtle Island. Part 3 returns

---

[2] As told in *Braiding Sweetgrass*, by Robin Wall Kimmer; also, from https://www.thecanadianencyclopedia.ca/en/article/turtle-island.

to Coast Salish territories, particularly Vancouver and Jedediah, with a focus on the period before and during WWI.

Within each section, I aim to contextualize my family's story with a three-part process: first place, then possession, and finally people. I begin by sharing what I have learned about the context and history of the places where my ancestors lived. Where possible, I share some of the voices of the Indigenous peoples who lived on the same lands that my ancestors have occupied; these voices speak truth to power so eloquently that their words ring through the centuries.

Next, I look at how my ancestors came to "own" the land they're on and what treaties did or did not exist on the land. I explore whatever historical records I am able to glean.

Finally, I share what I have been able to glean about my specific ancestors' lives: where they were born, whom they married, and anything we know about what they said, wrote, or did in their lives. I aim to honour their journeys and struggles. I look for ways to understand how they related to place and to colonization from their own perspectives.

As you read through this account, you may find that the connections I make between place, my ancestors, and colonization are interesting, inspiring, or curiosity-inducing. You also may find that some of these narratives are awkward, colonizing, or a bit over the top.

Whatever your reaction, thank you for reading, questioning, and engaging with this work. I'd love to hear from you.

Mali Bain
Vancouver, BC
August 2019

Background:
A Place-Based Family History

Why is this place-based approach to my family history important to me? I recommend reading this section only if you'd like a slightly more academic perspective on why I've undertaken this very personal, narrative work.

I see family history research as a very preliminary "step zero" toward understanding where I come from—and thus who I am—as part of finding ways to "unsettle the settler" within myself. I was encouraged in this approach by authors such as C. Haig-Brown[3] and Paulette Regan,[4] who have suggested that individuals look for personal historical and present-day connections to Indigenous peoples as a preliminary step toward unsettling. Sharing my family history within a place-based framework allows me to connect myself and my ancestors to place in the spirit of "all my relations."[5]

The approach I've taken to combining place, possession, and people is inspired by the work of Victoria Freeman.[6] Like Freeman, when I began the work of personal and family research, I had an unspoken sense that my ancestors "were essentially decent and well-intentioned people ... [and] had simply inherited the aftermath of an already

---

3   Haig-Brown, C. (2006). *With Good Intentions: Euro-Canadian and Aboriginal relations in colonial Canada*. Vancouver: UBC Press.
4   Regan, Paulette. (2011). *Unsettling the Settler Within*. Vancouver: UBC Press.
5   In the spirit of Robin Wall Kimmer, *Braiding Sweetgrass*.
6   Freeman, Victoria. (2000). *Distant Relations: How My Ancestors Colonized North America*. Hanover, New Hampshire: Steerforth Press.

accomplished dispossession."[7] Recognizing in myself and my family the assumptions named by Freeman and others, I was compelled to explore my family history in detail to understand when and how my ancestors' lives were shaped by colonialism. As part of my research, I began to ask questions about family connections with place and colonization; I read or re-read books related to my family history,[8] as well as the history of many parts of Turtle Island.

Language

Before diving in, a few points on language. My intention in this work is to identify and use, where possible, place names that have been in use since "time immemorial." When Europeans came to Turtle Island (North America), they decided to assign names to the features, landmarks, and bodies of water they found. Did they ask for the local names and then, when unable to pronounce them, just shake their heads and go for an alternate? Or, more likely, did they look at their own maps and decide that those things "discovered" but not yet labelled must be labelled? Most of the commonly used names that mark the mountains, streams, valleys, and islands on Turtle Island are names of "dead white men" who, in most cases, never actually set foot on the stream/river/mountain/island named after them. Others, like the word Canada, are derivations or mispronunciations of Indigenous words for places[9].

I use the term settler to describe non-Indigenous people such as myself, who are descendants of immigrants to Turtle Island at any

---

[7] Ibid, p. xvi.
[8] For a list of some of my most frequently cited sources, see 'Recommended Reading.'
[9] Origin of the Name Canada, https://www.canada.ca/en/canadian-heritage/services/origin-name-canada.html.

point in history. I use the term to remind myself and the reader of the ways that present-day Canada and the United States were set up as "settler colonies" of the British, French, and Spanish. I also use the term to refer to more recent newcomers to Canada.

I use the term Indigenous rather than Aboriginal or Indian, except where the original text uses other terms. "Indian" was the term erroneously given to residents of Turtle Island by early European colonizers who were attempting to sail to India. It is geographically incorrect and often has a pejorative connotation. Until recently, Aboriginal is the term that the Canadian government used to refer to the First Nations, Métis, and Inuit peoples. Aboriginal has identified a relationship to the Canadian state, rather than a connection to Indigenous culture and community. Since the 1970s, the term Indigenous has been adopted by international Indigenous movements as part of a global movement for rights, for example in the UN Declaration on the Rights of Indigenous Peoples.

Many, Many Limitations

This work is not necessarily representative of any broader truth or context for others on the same lands or even at the same time as my ancestors. What I share is a very thin, two-dimensional slice of a dynamic, complex set of stories about the past.

The research and learning shared rely on accounts that are written in English, recorded on paper, and thus exclude the oral histories passed down from generation to generation in Indigenous communities. When directly discussing Indigenous nations, I looked for sources from their modern nations. I sought permission for any stories shared.

Readers may note inaccuracies, misrepresentations, or grossly colonial assumptions in this work; I know I have. As I've gone through this process, the sources, stories, assumptions, and even questions asked throughout have continued to reveal my own "marination" in colonization.

There are inherent contradictions in the structure of this work. This work is inspired and held together by my own ancestry, so while I aim to start each section with a place-based lens, this work in its very structure still centres the settler narrative.

Through the process of doing this research, compiling sources and writing, I've begun the process of learning more about the places of my ancestors. I've continued to identify and unlearn some of my own assumptions and tendencies. My critical side has paused me in this work for months—over a year, at one point— halted by the realization that what I am writing still comes from the same colonial traditions that I am pointing out and trying to subvert.

I share what I have written with trepidation, sure that others wiser than myself, and likely future versions of myself, will see within this text assumptions, biases, and contradictions that are as yet not apparent to me. My hope is that I will soon have other books to read that continue to expand and deepen place-based family history.

Part 1.
Journeys to One Small Private Island

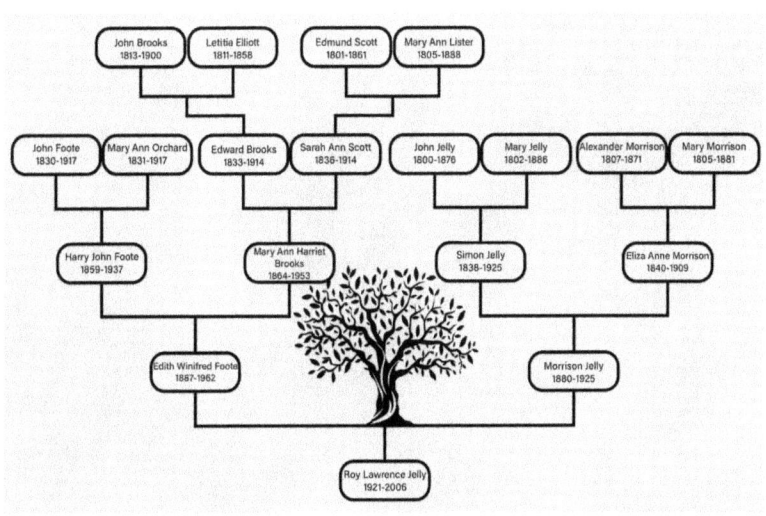

Jelly Family Tree.

1. Unceded Territories: And the Place Called Jedediah Island

This story begins on a small island off the Sunshine Coast: an island currently known as Jedediah Island.[10] Jedediah is part of the traditional territory of the Tla'amin Nation and was also accessed by other groups, including the Qualicum, Comox, Sechelt, Squamish, Nanoose, and the Te'mexw Treaty Association.[11]

Jedediah is an island of more than 700 acres located between Vancouver Island[12] and the Sunshine Coast in British Columbia. It's close enough to see as a spot on the horizon from Wreck Beach in Vancouver, and far enough to require a one-hour powerboat journey from either Parksville or Pender Harbour. The island is now a marine park[13] and a popular destination for sailboats and kayak tourers.

Multiple middens[14] on Jedediah suggest that the island was a valuable food-gathering site, likely to have been used for harvesting and drying clams during the summer months.

---

[10] I was unable to find an Indigenous name for the island known as Jedediah.
[11] Jedediah Island Marine Park: Background Document, http://www.env.gov.bc.ca/bcparks/explore/parkpgs/jedediah_is/jedediah-marine-bgdoc.pdf?v=1533233637534.
[12] I have not been able to source an Indigenous term for all of Vancouver Island, as it is a part of the territory of many nations.
[13] Jedediah was made a marine park in 1995 after a community-wide fundraising campaign purchased the island from its last beloved owner, Mary Palmer. Her history of the island, Jedediah Days, shares the stories of the several decades she spent on Jedediah.
[14] Middens are places where domestic waste has been piled over time and are indications of human activity. On the coast of BC, middens often consist of shells and other artifacts from daily food consumption.

Location of Jedediah Island.[15]

Archaeological research has uncovered 10 areas with significant evidence of human usage, as well as fish weirs.

A brief history posted by BC Parks says, "traditional use by First Nations after the arrival of the first European settlers is largely

---

[15] Map of Jedediah's location by Jitan Dahal.

unknown but would likely have decreased." Early European visitors and settlers would have encountered Indigenous peoples arriving on the island to continue the summer harvesting and fishing that they had been doing for thousands of years.

The earliest European visitors to the island are not recorded but would likely have arrived in the late 1700s or early 1800s. At that time, the British colonial government, and later the Dominion of Canada, issued documentation that recognized Indigenous title.

The Royal Proclamation of October 7, 1763, issued by the British Crown,[16] describes very clearly the limits of the rights of the royal government in relation to any unceded lands:

> We do therefore, with the Advice of our Privy Council, declare it to be our Royal Will and Pleasure, that ... no Governor or Commander in Chief in any of our other Colonies or Plantations in America do ... pass Patents for ... any Lands whatever, which, not having been ceded to or purchased by Us as aforesaid, are reserved to the said Indians, or any of them.

In effect, the Proclamation confirmed that all land must be considered Indigenous land until ceded by treaty to the Crown. The Proclamation language prevented colonial governments from granting any unceded or unpurchased land to individual British subjects. Land transfer could only happen through an official system of public purchases, for example through treaty, by colonial governments. This proclamation is the basis for Indigenous rights and a nation-to-nation relationship between First Nations and the government of Canada.

---

[16] This was then enshrined within section 25 of the Canadian Constitution in 1982.

Before we return to Jedediah Island, a few pieces of context. The overall Indigenous population on Turtle Island (North America) had decreased enormously since the arrival of the first Europeans. While estimates of population prior to contact vary from 2 million to 10 million people[17], there is no question that Indigenous populations plummetted due in large part to contact with colonizers and the spread of diseases never before experienced on Turtle Island, such as smallpox, measles, and influenza. For Turtle Island, this would have meant a population decline from 10 million people to 0.5 million within just one hundred years. On Captain George Vancouver's visit to Puget Sound in 1792, he records deserted villages, abandoned fishing boats, and human remains "promiscuously scattered about the beach, in great numbers."[18] It's staggering to imagine the scale of this devastation caused by the colonizers who arrived before Vancouver.

The result was that, in many parts of Turtle Island, land that had been cultivated for thousands of years was left "empty", which later naturally reforested. Recent studies[19] estimate that 56 million hectares, roughly the size of France, were reforested as a result of the decimation of the population.

---

[17] These statistics are debated in part because they are hard to comprehend, representing much higher mortality rates than those even of the Black Death in Europe, for example. Estimates here as cite in Haines, M.R. and Steckel, R.H. A Population History of North America. Cambridge University Press (2000), p. 13.
[18] As quoted in Mann, Charles C. 1491: New Revelations of the Americas Before Columbus. Knopf (2005). P. 110.
[19] "America Colonisation 'cooled Earth's climate'" – Jonathon Amos, BBC Science Correspondent. https://www.bbc.com/news/science-environment-47063973. Accessed Feb 15, 2019.

Across Canada, the British colonial government had, to varying extents, signed agreements or treaties with Indigenous peoples (more on those soon!). However, in BC, and on Jedediah Island, that important step was omitted. For the vast majority of British Columbia, treaties were not negotiated between the government and Indigenous peoples[20].

As of the early 1800s, the colony of Vancouver Island was the farthest west in then-British North America. In the early 1850s, then-governor James Douglas, whose wife was part Cree, had signed a set of treaties on southern Vancouver Island with Indigenous nations. These treaties are today called the "Douglas Treaties."

However, in 1858, the context completely changed with the Fraser Gold Rush. Suddenly, tens of thousands of white men, primarily from the United States, came in huge numbers up to Victoria and mainland British Columbia. In an effort to maintain British control of the land, the government created the Colony of BC to cover all of British Columbia and Vancouver Island. At the same time, the British colonial administration withdrew financial support for the treaty-making process. The combined effect significantly undermined Indigenous-settler relationships in BC. Without signing treaties or agreements, the government allowed settlement and began issuing "title deeds" for land all across the area.

---

[20] The exceptions are the Douglas treaties, discussed below, the Treaty 8 area in the Peace River region, and the "modern" agreements such as the Nisga'a Final Agreement and the Tsawwassen Treaty. Aboriginal Title in British Columbia, https://indigenousfoundations.arts.ubc.ca/aboriginal_title/.

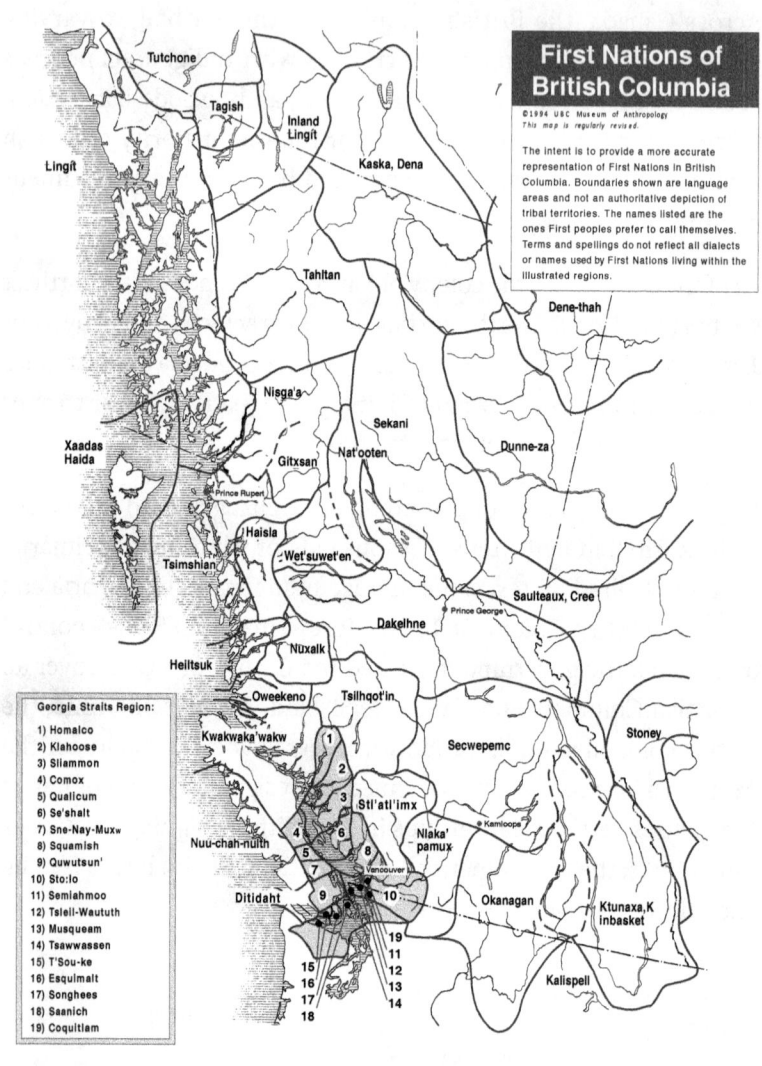

Map of British Columbia First Nations.[21]

---

[21] From UBC Museum of Anthropology.

The BC government's act of claiming and then selling land on the BC coast contravenes statements made in the Royal Proclamation. Jedediah Island, and most of BC, had never been "ceded to or purchased by" the Colony of British Columbia. Yet in 1890 the Government of British Columbia issued a title deed for Jedediah without even a gesture towards a negotiation, settlement, or discussion with the local nations. Like most land in British Columbia, this puts Jedediah in the category of "unceded Indigenous land"—in other words, stolen land[22].

It's not as though Indigenous people could themselves lawfully claim ownership of land such as Jedediah. The land grants allowed settlement and the "right to homestead" and were primarily intended for white settlers.

During Governor Douglas's tenure, Indigenous peoples were technically able to pre-empt land and thus potentially acquire their own land back. In 1863, a BC Indigenous man attempted to purchase Crown land at a public sale. General Moody was "shocked" but could see no reason to resist. After Governor Douglas retired a year later, Joseph Trutch took over the role responsible for Indigenous relations and settler land development in BC. By 1870, he and others made sure the Homesteading Act was amended to clarify that pre-emption rights did not apply to Indigenous peoples. In other words, settlers could homestead and lay claim to up to 320 acres, but "Indians" did not have the same rights to select and pre-empt land.

---

[22] In BC there are still vast swaths of land called Crown land. It's quite ironic, it seems to me, that land never ceded to any "Crown" is given the most colonial of all names.

By 1876, Indigenous peoples in BC were under the constrictions of the Indian Act,[23] which outlined the relationship between Indigenous and non-Indigenous peoples in Canada. The Act considered Indigenous peoples to be "savages" and therefore non-citizens. As non-citizens, "Indians" were unable to vote or hold private property and, thus, it would have been almost impossible to "pre-empt" or purchase the land of Jedediah.

In the early part of the 20th century, decades after my ancestors purchased Jedediah, the government of BC had set in place the McKenna-McBride Commission. The commission was set up from 1910 to 1912 "to investigate the condition of Indian Affairs in the Province of British Columbia and to settle all differences between Our Governments of Canada and British Columbia respecting Indian lands and Indian affairs generally in the said Province." This goal is laughably ambitious for a two-person commission composed of two settlers.

However, despite this stated vision, the Commission's mandate was limited to exploring the size of reserves allocated to Indigenous peoples in BC. They were to "investigate and make recommendations regarding the lands reserved for Indians ... and regarding such additional lands as might appear to be required for the necessary use of the Indians of the Province."[24]

---

[23] For more on the Indian Act, see '21 Things you may not know about the Indian Act' by Bob Joseph or this useful resource: https://indigenousfoundations.arts.ubc.ca/the_indian_act/.

[24] The Union of British Columbia Indian Chiefs has transcribed and made available the entire McKenna-McBride commission here: https://www.ubcic.bc.ca/mckenna_mcbride_royal_commission.

An Indigenous nation or band was allocated small portions of land through the "reserve system"—land held at 10 acres (or less) for each family, as a part of government-selected sites.[25] These government-allocated parcels, or reserves, were (and are) not actually owned by individual families but rather held by the Crown "in trust" for Indigenous peoples. There is a strongly paternalistic underpinning to this relationship, as Indigenous peoples are treated as incapable of managing their own lands judiciously. Reserves are defined in the Indian Act as follows:

> *Reserves are held by Her Majesty for the use and benefit of the respective bands for which they were set apart, and subject to this Act and to the terms of any treaty or surrender, the Governor in Council may determine whether any purpose for which lands in a reserve are used or are to be used is for the use and benefit of the band.*[26]

The McKenna-McBride Commission travelled across British Columbia, creating a total of 27 volumes of written records as well as summary reports. While I was not able to find commission records directly pertaining to Jedediah, I did find records from Thormanby Island, a slightly smaller island just off the Sunshine Coast about 12 kilometers from Jedediah. Below is a verbatim transcript of an interaction pertaining to Thormanby Island:

JOE LA DALLY MAKES AN APPLICATION.

MR. COMMISSIONER CARMICHAEL: What do you want?

---

25 "Property Rights" in Aboriginal People: History of Discriminatory Laws, 1987. http://publications.gc.ca/Collection-R/LoPBdP/BP/bp175-e.htm. Also "Indian Reservations" in Stó:lō Heritage Trust. (2001). A Stó:lō-Coast Salish Historical Atlas. (K. T. Carlson, Ed.). Vancouver: Douglas & McIntyre, p. 94.
26 Indian Act, Section 18(1), accessed at https://laws-lois.justice.gc.ca/eng/acts/I-5/FullText.html.

A. *I want to get a piece of land—I have been wanting a piece of land for a long time, and now that you are here I want to ask for it. I wrote to Ottawa for a piece of land and I got no answer that Mr. Byrne would help me, and then I was told to wait for this Commission. I have no land at all—I am staying at Skookumchuck, but the land that I have my houses on does not belong to me—I have no land of my own with my family.*

Q. *Are you a member of this Band?*

A. *I belong to this band.*

Q. *Whereabouts is this piece of land that you want to get?*

A. *There is a piece of land where my parents lived and that is the piece of land that I want.*

Q. *Where is it?*

A. *On Thormanby Island near Welcome Passage.*

MR. COMMISSIONER MACDOWALL: *The whole of that Island has been sold and taken up by whitemen.*

MR. COMMISSIONER CARMICHAEL: *Were there any improvements on that Island?*

A. *It was an old camping ground for years, and my father was buried there.*

Q. *When were you there last?*

A. *I have not been there lately. I am afraid to go there because I thought I had no right there.*

Q. Is there just the one grave there or are there more?

A. I know of eleven bodies there myself, but I don't know how many there are altogether. It used to be an old fort years ago when the Indians used to have their battles and it used to be fenced.

Q. That appears to be all taken up, and I don't see that there is any possibility of our being able to get it for you; but there was an Indian here a few moments ago who said that he would be willing to have some other Indian come and help him improve his reserve—perhaps you could go there.

WITNESS: It is true what you have said, but I want to find out what I could do with those graves that are there.

MR. COMMISSIONER CARMICHAEL: We will remember that very carefully when we get back to Victoria.[27]

It is difficult to read this text, to note the clear distress of the applicant, who was unable to access his own father's grave; and to read the simple and matter-of-fact responses of the commissioners.

After reading this section, my father asked what the Commissioners actually did in Victoria, given that they promised they would remember "very carefully" the man's request in Victoria. While the Commissioners did submit a report to the government, I was not able to find any mention of Thormanby Island in the final reports. The summary report did briefly note that "on every occasion where meetings were held with the Indians, they expressed their views freely on questions of administration."

---

[27] Ibid.

On Thormanby Island, as on Jedediah, the approach of the BC colonial government was to assume the settlement rights and needs of the settlers first.

It wasn't entirely out of the ordinary in that era for groups of white settlers to set up shop on remote locations on the coast of BC. British Columbia, from the perspective of the rest of Turtle Island, was the "west beyond the west," "the place where we sense anything may happen."[28]

The desire for a more isolated lifestyle, which may have motivated the Foote's purchase of Jedediah, was shared by other settler groups at the time. There were several fascinating group ventures in the late nineteenth and early twentieth centuries.

For example, in 1901 a group of Finnish coal miners oppressed by coal baron James Dunsmuir became frustrated by their lot. Dunsmuir had been known for requiring workers to purchase goods at expensive company stores, and at one point imposing a 30 percent wage cut on his already low-paid mining employees.[29] Inspired by Finnish utopian Matti Kurikka, a group of miners in Nanaimo decided to get out of the coal mines and start a new life in a utopian commune. They chose a location much more remote than Jedediah: an island in Kwakwaka'wakw territory, now known as Malcolm Island,[30] 300 kilometres north of Nanaimo, off the eastern end of Vancouver Island. At that point, the island was accessible only by several days'

---

[28] Brown, Justine (1995). *All Possible Worlds: Utopian Experiments in British Columbia*, p. 13.
[29] Barman, Jean (1996). *The West Beyond the West: A History of British Columbia* (Rev. ed.). Toronto: University of Toronto Press, p. 122.
[30] I was not able to identify the Kwakwaka'wakw name for the island known as Malcolm Island.

boat ride from Nanaimo or Vancouver. Starting with just five people, the community grew, one idealist at a time. Over a few years they expanded to hundreds, built a community hall, shared communal meals, and established universal daycare.

Unfortunately, a combination of a disastrous fire at the community hall, leadership issues, and major financial difficulties meant the end of the utopian vision. By 1904, the community society disbanded and separated; still, many residents of the original commune stayed, and to this day Sointula has an unusually high ratio of Finnish saunas to households.

Around the same time, in an even more remote location, a group of Danes created the colony of Cape Scott. Set up in 1897, this community was also inspired by a visionary leader. For many years, the Danes attempted to prepare fields, build homes, and build roads. They even built a community hall and hosted a community dance. Like the Sointula colony, the experiment ended in disaster: the dyke they carefully built was destroyed almost immediately by a severe storm, and after years of painstaking construction of a corduroy road (now the Cape Scott Trail), the government reneged on its promise to build a road to meet theirs. With limited land and without access to markets, the last residents of the settlement left Cape Scott by 1909.

By comparison with these examples, my ancestors' sojourn on Jedediah Island was small and rather private—just a small island, just a single home, a mere day's journey up the coast.

2. One Small "Private" Island, 1890–1910s

Harry John Foote	Mary Ann Harriet Brooks
1859–1937	1864–1953
Edith Winifred (Winnie) Foote	Morris Jelly
1887–1962	1880–1925
Roy Jelly	Marjorie Edwards
1921–2006	1923–2016

The Foote family's connection with Jedediah island began in 1890, soon after Harry and Mary Ann Foote moved by horse and buggy across the country from Portage la Prairie, Manitoba. They arrived in Vancouver—part of Coast Salish territory, though they didn't recognize it as such—with four children, including my great-grandmother Winnie. While living on Coast Salish territory they had two more children, Myrtle and Lister.[31]

When the Footes arrived in Vancouver, they assumed they had the right to purchase land. As non-Indigenous citizens, they were free to purchase as much land as they wished, anywhere on the coast.

---

[31] They lived first on 10th Ave and then built a home on the southeast corner of 12th & Alberta in Vancouver. More on their story and life in Vancouver in the last chapter.

View across Home Bay to Foote homestead. Photo: Andy Gullins, August 2018.

Harry Foote purchased Jedediah from George Stubbins, who had obtained it as a Crown Land Grant earlier that year, in 1890. Though the lands were Indigenous and had never been "ceded" or legally transferred to the British Columbia government, Harry claimed "ownership" of the islands with the stroke of a pen and the exchange of funds in Vancouver. The title deed for Jedediah, given to the first owner by the government, would have read something like this:

> *Victoria, by the Grace of God, of the United Kingdom of Great Britain and Ireland, Queen, Defender of the Faith, and so forth.*
>
> *To Whom these presents shall come, Greeting:*

> We give and grant ____ his heirs and assigns ... to have and to hold the said Parcel or Plot of Land and all and singular the premises hereby granted ...

This title deed text was justified by colonial jurisdiction over all of what was called British Columbia.

There are a few pieces of Harry Foote's title deed which are important to note. At the time when Harry and Mary Ann purchased Jedediah, Indigenous peoples did not have access to their traditional lands because of the encroaching settlers; in addition, they were prevented by law from purchasing the lands that they had lived on for generations. Finally, the land that was sold was not legally owned by the Province of British Columbia at the time.

As I was putting together this work, I shared an early version with one of my aunts. She wrote back with an insightful metaphor. She suggested that purchasing land in BC was a bit like purchasing a used car, and then later finding out that the seller doesn't have clear title to the car—either because it was owned by a bank (as a loan security) or was stolen. Even though you bought the car in good faith, you could not keep it—and the process of getting the money back would not be guaranteed.

If land is seen as a possession and as property, as is common in settler colonial culture, then the metaphor is helpful. If colonization was about stealing land, then the way to reconcile is to deal with these "stolen goods." The complex part is that there are thousands of such deals in BC, and they go back hundreds of years. The conversation becomes even more complex if land in itself is not seen as something to be "owned" and sold and traded, but rather a common good, a set of relationships with land, water, food, and ceremony.

Nevertheless, my great-great grandfather, Harry Foote, was able to purchase pieces of paper which gave him title to Jedediah Island in 1890. Starting in 1907, when their youngest, Lister, was 13 years old, Harry cleared land and began to build a home at what they called Home Bay, on Jedediah Island.

One can only imagine Harry in 1907, on the big day, the journey day. In the next year he planned to build a house on a small island off the coast of BC. The house-building cargo would have been piled high in burlap-covered stacks, including a cast-iron stove, stacks of wood, and roofing tin.

While Harry owned a boat for transport of his own family, for this big load it is likely he would have put his construction materials onto a larger boat or barge. The Union Steamship Company had a fleet of sturdy boats that serviced the small islands, logging camps, and remote communities of the coast from the early 1900s,[32] with a stopping-point on nearby Lasqueti. Just as with his Vancouver home, he would probably have hired

House at Jedediah, with extensive docks.

---

[32] Until 1923, when a ship struck a rock in Tucker Bay and the company's service to Lasqueti Island ended.

help to build the house—local men who could come for a few months of work to set up the basics.

Map of Jedediah Island Marine Park today.[33]

---

[33] From Jedediah Island Marine Park Reserve; http://www.env.gov.bc.ca/bcparks/explore/parkpgs/jedediah_is/.

Harry's sons were probably there to help him. Ed, carrying the basket with nourishment for the journey: four loaves of bread, ham, a thick slab of butter. Cedric might have double-checked the pallets of wood protecting the wood stove. Harry might have been anticipating the many hours of sailing ahead, the many supplies and workers he needed to arrange, the logistics and challenges of building a home on the bluffs above Home Bay.

They finished the Jedediah house by 1908: a two-storey, wood-frame house, perched on stilts of beach logs above the protected Home Bay. The front had tall narrow windows into the front room and sitting rooms, and upstairs were three bedrooms, with a dormer window facing the view out across Home Bay. Across the width of the house was a long welcoming veranda, with stairs twisting down the bluffs toward the wharf. The house still stands today, grey wood weathered from over a hundred years of storms, wind, and seagull splatter.

House on Jedediah Island. Photo: Andy Gullins, 2018.

Their existence on Jedediah was most definitely remote. The island was, at that time, a several-hour boat ride from the nearest hospital on the Sunshine Coast and a day's sail from Vancouver. The family's boat, Mary, transported the family from Vancouver to Jedediah. Whoever was on the island at the time was responsible for making the long trip to pick up the adults and kids for summer holidays. They docked somewhere in False Creek, passing under the present-day Granville Street Bridge.

Home Bay with the tide out. Photo: Andy Gullins, August 2018.

While Home Bay was scenic, it had one significant flaw: the entire shallow bay drained at low tide, making boat transport possible only near high tide. In later years, when Harry Foote convinced Canada Post to set up a mail stop on Jedediah, the government actually paid for the construction of a dock and long, narrow wharf—effective only at mid- to high tides, of course.

They developed an extensive garden, planted an orchard with several varieties of apples, and imported sheep.

Morris Jelly, my great-grandfather, on Jedediah Island.

My great-great grandparents Harry and Mary Ann Foote may have been completely unaware of the restrictions placed on Indigenous peoples by the Indian Act, or of the statements being made to the McKenna-McBride Commission about land just a few kilometres from Jedediah. They may have met and encountered Indigenous peoples on Jedediah and/or on the coast; however, there are few clues to the types of interactions these homesteaders may have had with Indigenous residents of the land.

My grandfather Roy Jelly recalled that he heard his grandmother, Mary Ann, speak "Indian" on a trip up the coast years later. This was most likely a reference to Chinook, the local trade language, which was known to whites as the "Indian language" and to Indigenous peoples as the "white man's language." While Mary Ann must have had connections and interactions with Indigenous peoples, I wasn't able to find any additional evidence of the Footes' connections to local Indigenous people.

Harry and Mary Ann spent many summers, and a few winters, on Jedediah. From 1908 to 1910, Jedediah was home to Harry and Mary's eldest daughter, Olive Olmstead, and her family. In the summer of 1910, the Olmsteads, Footes, and Jellys moved in more permanently, apparently even setting up a little general store on the island.

Before delving further into their stories on Jedediah, the next section explores where Harry Foote came from before arriving on Coast Salish territory with enough money to buy a private island.

3. Ouentironk (Lake Simcoe): And Treaties

Harry Foote was born in England and first immigrated as a child to a town called Sutton on the south shore of a lake called Ouentironk, or "beautiful water," by the Wyandot or Wendat peoples. Settlers called it Lake Simcoe.[34]

The south shore was within the lands of the Wendat (or Huron) Confederacy, which had been formed by four groups in the late 1600s and early 1700s. By the 1800s, the population had been decimated by smallpox carried by European immigrants, as well as by significant attacks from rival Iroquois. Survivors wintered on Gahoedoe, or Christian, an island in Georgian Bay, before fleeing to present-day Wendake, near Montreal.

The only agreement I was able to find was a one written one agreement between Indigenous residents and settlers from 1760, which the Huron signed with British Brigadier General James Murray":

> THESE are to certify that the CHIEF of the HURON tribe of Indians, having come to me in the name of His Nation, to submit to His BRITANNICK MAJESTY, and make Peace, has been received under my Protection, with his whole Tribe; and henceforth no English Officer or party is to molest, or interrupt them in returning to their Settlement at LORETTE; and they are received upon the same terms with the Canadians, being allowed the free Exercise

---

[34] Lake Simcoe was named after the father of John Simcoe, the first Lieutenant General of Upper Canada.

of their Religion, their Customs, and Liberty of trading with the English: recommending it to the Officers commanding the Posts, to treat them kindly.

Given under my hand at Longueil, this 5th day of September, 1760.

By the Genl's Command,

JOHN COSNAN, JA. MURRAY.

Adjut. Genl.

This peace agreement covered "kindness" but did not make specific land concessions or agreements.

Just a few years later, in the summer of 1764, came an important turning point: the Treaty of Niagara. The British government called Indigenous chiefs and leaders to gather in Niagara. In total approximately 2,000 chiefs attended, traveling from as far as Mississippi, Nova Scotia, and Hudson Bay. Sir William Johnson, representative of the British, stated:

> *Brothers of the Western Nations, Sachems, Chiefs and Warriors; You have now been here for several days, during which time we have frequently met to renew and Strengthen our Engagements and you have made so many Promises of your Friendship and Attachment to the English that there now remains for us only to exchange the great Belt of the Covenant Chain that we may not forget our mutual Engagements. I now therefore present you the great Belt by which I bind all your Western Nations together with the English, and I desire that you will take fast hold of the same, and never let it slip, to which end I desire that after you have shewn this Belt to all Nations you will fix one end of it with the Chipeweighs at St. Marys*

[Michilimackinac] *whilst the other end remains at my house, and moreover I desire that you will never listen to any news which comes to any other Quarter. If you do it, it may shake the Belt.* [35]

The wampum exchanged, often called the "two-row wampum," is described below by Robert A. Williams, Jr., a legal academic and member of the Lumbee tribe:

> *When the Haudenosaunee first came into contact with the European nations, treaties of peace and friendship were made. Each was symbolized by the Gus-Wen-Tah, or Two Row Wampum. There is a bed of white wampum which symbolizes the purity of the agreement. There are two rows of purple, and those two rows have the spirit of your ancestors and mine. There are three beads of wampum separating the two rows and they symbolize peace, friendship and respect. These two rows will symbolize two paths or two vessels, travelling down the same river together. One, a birch bark canoe, will be for the Indian people, their laws, their customs and their ways. The other, a ship, will be for the white people and their laws, their customs, and their ways. We shall each travel the river together, side by side, but in our own boat. Neither of us will try to steer the other's vessel.*[36]

This was the basis on which the Crown began negotiations, before any treaties had been signed. In many ways, there is a note of significant hope here: the spirit of the two-row wampum, in which

---

[35] As quoted in John Borrows, Wampum at Niagara, p.5. https://www.sfu.ca/~palys/Borrows-WampumAtNiagara.pdf.

[36] Williams, R.A., Jr. (1994). Linking Arms Together: Multicultural Constitutionalism in a North American Indigenous Vision of Law and Peace. *California Law Review*, vol. 82(4), 981–1049.

nations "travel the river together, side by side, but in our own boat,"[37] demonstrates a foundation of peace, respect, and even friendship.

Despite this precedent, settlement in Ontario, and in fact all across Turtle Island, was predicated upon the concept of terra nullius, which translates literally as "nobody's land". Legally, this meant that governments could grant land, mineral, and other rights without consulting with Indigenous peoples, let alone recognizing their inherent rights. Culturally, this same set of ingrained assumptions allows historical accounts of Canada or Turtle Island to tell stories of "frontier life" and of individual Indigenous peoples who entered settler life without reference to the structures, cultures, and governance structures that had existed, and continue to exist, across Turtle Island.[38]

Terra nullius was in some ways an expansion of the "doctrine of discovery," which was established through Roman Catholic Papal Bulls in the 1400s, and confirmed in the early 1800s in the United States (though not as widely used in Canada). The concept was that a "discovery" gave exclusive title to those who made it. In other words, by "discovering" the so-called New World, Europeans instantly gained rights to land that had been occupied by the Indigenous peoples they "discovered."

The implications of this concept are deadly serious. Throughout the 19th, 20th and 21st centuries, colonial governments continue to legitimize rule over Indigenous territories by using precedent that

---

[37] Ibid.
[38] One example of this is *Roughing It in the Bush*, by Susanna Moodie, who depicts "Indian" people she came to know as subjects of humorous stories and/or grateful for the kindnesses of settlers.

amounts to no more than a refined version of "finders keepers"—as long as the finders are European, that is.

In its 45th Call to Action, the 2015 Final Report of the Truth and Reconciliation Commission of Canada proposed a Royal Proclamation of Reconciliation which would "build on the Royal Proclamation of 1763 and the Treaty of Niagara of 1764," and would include a commitment to "repudiate concepts used to justify European sovereignty over Indigenous lands and peoples such as the Doctrine of Discovery and terra nullius."[39]

Through a combination of concepts such as terra nullius and the Doctrine of Discovery, settlers on Turtle Island tried to justify their occupation of the land. In what became known as southern Ontario, the colonial government continued to issue titles to land, despite the Treaty of Niagara.

Throughout the 1800s, the government did not sign treaties to the land south of Lake Simcoe. In 1923, recognizing this lack of clear title to land already settled, the government struck a three-person commission. The "Williams Commission" investigated the issue and confirmed the validity of Indigenous claims to the land of much of central and southern Ontario.[40] In what must be record time for a Canadian commission, the commissioners drafted and had treaties signed by the end of that same year. The treaties were written by the Canadian government and did not involve negotiation over the terms: identical agreements were signed by the Chippewa and Mississauga nations within a month of each other in 1923. The

---

[39] See https://nctr.ca/records/reports/.
[40] https://www.thecanadianencyclopedia.ca/en/article/williams-treaties, accessed September 2018.

treaty with the Chippewa of Christian Island, Georgina Island, and Rama included one-time payments only: $25 each to individuals and a paltry sum of $233,000 for the huge swaths of land near Lake Simcoe and other areas.

As Thomas King said about treaty rights:

> *A great many people in Turtle Island believe that Canada and the United States, in a moment of inexplicable generosity, gave treaty rights to Native people as a gift. Of course, anyone familiar with the history of Indians in Turtle Island knows that Native people paid for every treaty right, and in some cases, paid more than once. The idea that either country gave First Nations something for free is horseshit.* [41]

In fact, my ancestors were the ones getting something basically for free: the land and place they came to settle.

---

[41] King, Thomas. *The Inconvenient Indian: A Curious Account of Native People in North America.*

4. East End London to Ouentironk (Lake Simcoe), 1870s

John Foote	Mary Ann Orchard
1830–1917	1831–1917
Harry John Foote	Mary Ann Harriet Brooks
1859–1937	1864–1953
Edith Winifred (Winnie) Foote	Morris Jelly
1887–1962	1880–1925
Roy Jelly	Marjorie Edwards
1921–2006	1923–2016

In the spring of 1870, on the other side of the Atlantic, in London, England, an 11-year-old Harry, his four siblings, and his parents packed their bags.

John Foote and Mary Ann Orchard had married in their hometown, Southhampton, in the south of England. They were well-to-do enough to warrant getting a professional photo taken of Mary Ann dressed in formal dark attire. Her face is serious, her eyes look to the corner of the room, and she's gripping the fabric of her dress. Her right hand rests on a stack of books, suggesting literacy or at least the semblance of such.

After about 18 years of marriage, in 1870 they were living in a district called Poplar, in the poor East End of London, which primarily serviced the docks.

Mary Orchard.[42]

During that time, several "emigration funds" were set up to permanently solve the problem of poverty, particularly in the East End, by shipping the poorest families out of the country entirely. One such endeavor was the East London Emigration Fund, which set up the emigration of more than 1,030 people to the "colonies"—primarily Canada. The fund was created by the Honorable Mrs. Hobart and supported by financial contributions from "other ladies of distinction." These upper-class families ensured that "before leaving London

---

42   Image from adfuquay on Ancestry.ca.

[the emigrants] were invited to tea, for the purpose of explaining to them the final arrangements made for their departure to and reception in Canada, each head of a family being called upon to sign a paper promising to pay the amount advanced for this passage and outfit, as soon as he should be able to do so."[43]

Given their circumstances and geography, it is likely that John and Mary Ann were beneficiaries of the East End Emigration Fund or something similar. They were seven of the 32,500 people who immigrated to Canada in that year[44]; over half of those immigrants were from the United Kingdom.

John and Mary Ann's five children are recorded, along with their ages, in the ledger of the sailing ship the St. Lawrence (see below). They and 145 fellow passengers spent just over a month confined on board. With five children from one to 15 years old, the voyage must have been quite memorable.

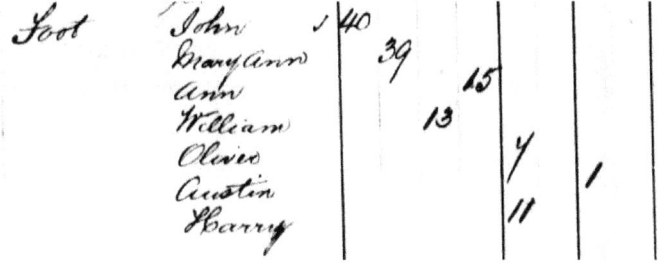

St. Lawrence ledger with Foot[e] names. Numbers listed are ages.[45]

---

[43] Kohli, Marjorie. "Immigrants to Canada". https://personal.uwaterloo.ca/marj/genealogy/reports/emigrationsoc.html. Accessed December 2018.
[44] As cited at http://jubilation.uwaterloo.ca/~marj/genealogy/reports/report1868.html.
[45] From Canadian Passenger Lists, 1865–1935. Library and Archives Canada; Ottawa, Ontario, Canada; Series: RG 76-C; Roll: C-4523. Accessed via ancestry.ca July 2019.

We don't know the terms under which John and Mary Ann gained access to land in Canada upon their arrival; they were one family of thousands arriving at the time, many of whom received land grants from the government.

John and Mary Ann arrived in Canada just three years after the 1867 British North America Act had created the Dominion of Canada, and thirteen years after the 1857 Gradual Civilization Act, a precursor to the Indian Act that created a system whereby "Indians" could give up all rights to Indigenous land in exchange for the right to vote.[46]

It is likely that in the journey from Toronto north to Sutton, on the shores of Ouentironk (Lake Simcoe), John and Mary Ann would have passed by the former centre point of Huron/Wendat history, what is now known as the "Mantle Site." This large town of 1,500 to 2,000 residents was the largest settlement of its kind in the area and had been in active use until the mid-1600s, several hundred years before their arrival.

While I do not know to what extent John and Mary Ann connected directly with contemporary Indigenous neighbours, they would probably have encountered Indigenous peoples in their goings-about in Sutton. Here's the account of elder Susan Hoeg (née Vernon) of the Georgina Island First Nation, located just north of Sutton:

> *In the late 1820s, the Indian Department of Upper Canada began to relocate the Lake Simcoe Indians. The Indians were blamed for destroying wildlife so they were encouraged to farm.*

---

[46] Only one Indigenous person voluntarily enfranchised under this Act.

> Snake Island was the first island the Indians settled on in Lake Simcoe. With more pressure to farm, they moved to the larger and more isolated Georgina Island. Only a few remained on Snake Island. The population on Georgina Island in 1876 was 131 ...
>
> [My grandfather] rowed across the lake in a boat he had built. Every week the supplies were shopped for in the nearby towns. Hours were spent carving ax handles, while my grandmother made beautiful baskets trimmed with sweet grass and porcupine quills. They would then take them to the villages and sell or trade them for food or clothes.[47]

Did John and Mary Ann trade for some of the ax handles or baskets? There are no records of these transactions, nor any way to know.

---

[47] From History of Georgina Island, Chippewas of Georgina Island. http://georginaisland.com/writing/history-of-georgina-island/.

John and Mary Ann's Sutton Homestead.[48]

As shown in a photograph of their homestead, Mary Ann herself is holding the hand of a young child—perhaps Austin, the youngest, born in England—near John, who sits nearby, hands on his knees. Annie, her oldest daughter, displays to the camera Lily, the "surprise" child, born in Canada when Mary Ann was 44 years old. William (Billy), the oldest son, stands in front of the porch with a resplendent moustache, holding a younger sibling. Standing on the left of the group is Harry, next-eldest son, his left hand on his hip—my ancestor and future occupant of Jedediah Island. Their modest wooden home is simply constructed, built in what appears to be a rural area.

---

[48] Image from adfuquay on Ancestry.ca.

John and Mary Anne and their family; Mary Anne Orchard in older age.[49]

John and Mary Anne Foote stayed the rest of their lives on the shores of Ouentironk (Lake Simcoe). Later photos, such as the one included here, depict John and Mary Ann, here seated with Anne Foote Thayer, their eldest daughter, standing, and Billy (William) Foote, their eldest son, standing to the right. It would have been around this time that Mary Ann had another portrait done, depicting an older, dignified woman with a persistently grave look.

John and Mary Ann's eldest daughter, Annie, lived in the area her whole life, and bore 10 children. She would have been residing in the area when, in 1923, nearly 50 years later, the colonial Canadian government signed the Williams Treaties discussed earlier.

---

49 ibid.

Harry Foote, John and Mary Ann's second-eldest son, didn't stay near Ouentironk: he went farther west, to Portage la Prairie.

5. Portage la Prairie

The land of Portage la Prairie in present-day Manitoba has been, since time immemorial, Ojibway and Cree land. The current townsite is on the edge of Long Plain, a site of buffalo and deer hunting.[50]

In the early days of the fur trade, Portage was established as Fort la Reine. As the name Portage suggests, it was a place where travellers moving by canoe had to portage from one river system to another. Fur traders would move their goods and canoes by land from the Assiniboine River to Lake Manitoba as part of their journey to Fort Dauphin, farther upstream.

In 1869, the Hudson's Bay Company sold 3.9 million square kilometres of land to the Canadian government. The only problem, of course, was that the Hudson's Bay Company didn't truly own the land it sold.

It wasn't until a few years later, in 1871, that the government signed Treaty 1 and Treaty 2 with Indigenous peoples in what is now the southern part of Manitoba. The Canadian government interpreted these treaties as "blanket extinguishment" of Indigenous title to the land; however, many legal cases since then have argued that the Indigenous signatories to the treaties, who came from oral traditions and ways of knowing, understood and passed on completely different interpretations of the texts. More on that later.[51]

---

[50] From Metis Museum http://www.metismuseum.ca/media/document.php/149153. Fort%20la%20Reine.pdf.
[51] For a good overview of land title, see https://indigenousfoundations.arts.ubc.ca/aboriginal_title/.

In the years since colonization, Manitoba had also become home to the Métis people. As the Métis Nation of Canada describes its origins,

> The advent of the fur trade in west central North America during the 18th century was accompanied by a growing number of mixed offspring of Indian women and European fur traders. As this population established distinct communities separate from those of Indians and Europeans and married among themselves, a new Aboriginal people emerged—the Métis people—with their own unique culture, traditions, language (Michif), way of life, collective consciousness and nationhood.[52]

After the Rupert's Land purchase, when the government attempted to survey the land and divide it up into square blocks, the Métis pushed back. Led by Louis Riel, they set up a provisional government and succeeded in negotiating with the newly formed Canadian government. The rebellion ended with the 1870 creation of the first post-Confederation province: Manitoba.

In the years after the 1870 uprisings, the government aimed to extinguish Métis title to land by allocating parcels of land to individual Métis through a series of government commissions in the 1870s and 1880s. These land allocations, known as scrip, required unwieldy processes and often allocated land far from the area of residence of Métis. Unscrupulous "scrip hunters" or "jobbers" often pressured Métis to sell the scrip for less than they were worth. Those pieces of scrip became an item of significant speculation in southern Manitoba for years to come—so much so that Winnipeg newspapers contained daily advertisements to buy and sell scrip. While records suggest that Métis heads of

---

[52] http://www.metisnation.ca/index.php/who-are-the-metis.

family sold their scrip quickly, there are few records remaining as to who originally picked up the scrip, who sold it, and how the purchased scrip was used.[53] The scrip process and speculation were met with considerable frustration from Métis communities in Manitoba and farther west.

There are others who have written much more about this: however, in early 1885, based on dissatisfaction with the land scrip process and with their overall treatment by the government, the Métis invited Louis Riel to head up what became known as the North West rebellion. This time, armed forces arrived via the newly constructed train and ended the rebellion. Riel gave himself up to the police; he was convicted of treason and hanged in 1885 in Regina.

---

[53] Gerhard Ens and Joe Sawchuck, New Peoples to New Nations: Aspects of Metis History and Identity p. 148.

6. Harry and Mary Ann: Ouentironk to Métis Land, 1880s

John and Mary Anne's son Harry—the same Harry who would eventually purchase Jedediah—moved west from Ouentirok to Manitoba in his early 20s. Harry probably arrived in Manitoba in the years after the first Métis rebellions and the creation of the province of Manitoba.

Soon after the social, charismatic Harry arrived in Portage la Prairie, he met a young woman who happened to share his mother's first name: Mary Ann. Mary Ann Harriet Brooks' family, like Harry's, came from Ontario and, before that, from England. On the next page is a photo of Mary Ann's mother, Sarah Anne Brooks (née Scott), wearing a determined gaze and finely trimmed headpiece. Sarah was born, raised, and married in Stratford on Avon, Ontario. In the 1870s Sarah and Edward Brook moved with their family, including Mary Ann and her twin sister Letitia, to Marquette, Manitoba, a tiny town between Winnipeg and Portage la Prairie. Edward Brooks was a carpenter/contractor, and he built what was known as the Brooks Block on Saskatchewan Avenue in Portage la Prairie.

Harry was slightly older, at 23, and Mary Ann was just 17 when they were married in 1882. Portage la Prairie had only 995 people in 1871, but by 1881 it had become a bustling small town of just over 4,000 people. During the early years of their marriage, Harry worked for a company that managed telephones. In 1884 there were only 18 telephones in the entire city!

Sarah Anne Brook (nee Scott) [54]

In the 1889 Winnipeg Free Press, under the section 'Portage La Prairie,' dated August 2, I found this note:

> *"Mr. N.F. Snider is fitting up the most westerly store in the Martin & Curtis building as an office. In short time he takes charge of the telegraph and telephone business at present managed by Foote & Snider. Harry Foote going into the insurance and real estate line."*

And so, Harry moved to real estate, associated with the firm Foote & Woodside on Main Street. As a real estate agent, Harry's role was to buy and sell land. This meant that he would have had frequent contact with discussions about the origin, ownership, and transfer of land in Portage la Prairie.

---

[54] Image from stark 2217 on Ancestry.ca.

When I first began researching Harry's history, I couldn't help but wonder if Harry Foote, as a real estate agent, had earned money in part through the sale of Métis land scrip. As it turns out, Harry moved into real estate at a time when it's likely that scrip sales were waning, though land speculation would continue in the area.

During his years in Portage la Prairie, Harry acquired some wealth. In 1890, he and his family of five children decided to move halfway across the country to Vancouver, where, upon arrival, he had the financial means to purchase land, including Jedediah Island.

Before following Harry farther West, though, it's important to trace the origins of another significant Jedediah family: the Jelly family.

7. The Jelly Connection: Jellyby, Ontario, 1800s

John Jelly 1800–1876	Mary Jelly 1802–1886
Simon Jelly 1838–1925	Eliza Ann Morrison 1838–1909
Morris Jelly 1880–1925	Edith Winifred (Winnie) Foote 1887–1962
Roy Jelly 1921–2006	Marjorie Edwards 1923–2016

One of the challenges of uncovering land history in Ontario is the layers of relationships between Indigenous peoples and settlers. Records suggest that the area where the Jellys settled may be in the territory of the Wendake-Nionwentsïo, Algonquin/Mississaugas, and Anishinabewaki.[55] It seems the area where the Jelly family arrived was covered by "Crawford's purchase"[56] of 1783. The Crawford purchase was an agreement between the Mississaugas, who had been in the area since 1700, and the Province of Quebec. The agreement gave British title to lands along the St. Lawrence and from there inland "as far as a man can travel in a day,"[57] which is interpreted as up to 50 km inland. This area would have included the land the Jellys settled on, which was about 25 kilometres from the river.

---

[55] Based on research compiled by https://native-land.ca/.
[56] https://www.ontario.ca/page/map-ontario-treaties-and-reserves#t2.
[57] https://www.thecanadianencyclopedia.ca/en/article/crawford-purchase.

Like the Footes, the Jelly family's history goes back to Ontario and, further back, to Great Britain. My first Jelly ancestor, John Jelly, came to Canada with his brother William and sister Anne from Belfast, Northern Ireland, in the 1820s. They bought land in 1827, and the original deed shows that the original land grant was made only a few decades earlier, in 1802. Similar to the rest of Canada, though, these land grants were only as valuable as the actual agreements underlying the piece of paper.

John Jelly and other early settlers made money from the sale of potash; when they cleared their land of timber and bush, the tons of ashes produced went downriver to potash factories along the St Lawrence.[58] The area became known as Jelly's Crossing for the obvious reason that the farm and railway tracks crossed there, at the site of the Jelly farm. The farm and area where the Jelly family settled in Canada is still to this day known as "Jellyby," today an hour's drive south of Ottawa.

A quick pause here to point out that an immigrant family arriving in the 1800s was welcomed to purchase and own land, and then have their family name associated with the land. At the same time, the people who had lived on those very same lands for thousands of years were not eligible for land grants, and the names they had used for generations were no longer used for waterways, lakes, or roads.

The Jelly family came to a landscape that had been forested for years, cleared and burned the trees, and sold the ash down the river; society accepted this practice, without questioning their right to destroy the forest. In early settler Canada, this was the kind of entrepreneurial activity that was appreciated enough to get your name on a road sign.

---

[58] http://www.lynmuseum.ca/2016/11/15/jellyby-forgotten-hamlet-elizabethtown/.

Jelly House, Jellyby. Photo: Mali Bain, January 2017.

When my sister and I went to visit the area in early 2017, we found a "Jellyby Rd" sign at an intersection in the middle of fields, almost completely deserted. Down the road, we found friendly neighbours who were happy to tell us more: Jellyby was at one point a station on the railway line between Brockville and Ottawa. With the station no longer in operation, the handful of farms remaining on either side of the tracks make up the hamlet of Jellyby. They directed us to one property in particular known as the Jelly Farm. We took a photo of what we believe is the Jelly home, where Morris Jelly, later to become an adventurer in Australia, grew up.

Jellyby Road sign. Photo: Mali Bain, January 2017.

The Jelly family were a colourful clan. The following story has no precise source, though it has been quoted several times in Jelly family histories:

> About 1860, the Jelly brothers were clearing land at the Jellyby property. According to Simon, he begged off sick and, after the others went to work, took the old shotgun, and walked through the bush to see the Morrison girl he was sweet on. Simon met her brothers and was standing on a log, talking to them, when the butt of the gun slipped off the log. His fingers slipped up the barrel, over the end, as the hammer hit the log. The gun discharged through his fingers, some of the pieces hitting him in the forehead. This entailed a trip to Brockville to a doctor, who suggested using a new drug called chloroform to put him out while he was treated. But Simon

woke up soon after it was administered. Simon reputedly told the doctor, "Give me a good shot of whiskey and go ahead."

Apparently, this mishap didn't do any harm to his chances with "the Morrison girl," Eliza Ann. A few years later, in 1862, he purchased 250 acres in Melancthon, now in the village of Shelburne, a one-week trip by horse from Jellyby. His poor luck continued after marriage. While doing statute labour (road maintenance in lieu of taxes), his team of horses bolted and he suffered a broken hip; after that incident, he needed to use a cane.

Simon Jelly.[59]

There are other hints of colour and scandal. For example, as reported in the 1972 Globe and Mail, "Bev Peterson, a 35-year-old farmer, says Jesse James was brought here by Simon Jelly, a man from the area who rode with the James gang for a time." While there's no evidence to back the rumour up, the Jelly stories do seem to make their way around.

Despite their rather infamous deeds, the property rights of the Irish Jelly family have never been seriously shaken. Since they first arrived in Canada, members of the Jelly family— at least the males—were

---

[59] Image from PattiAMcCurdy on Ancestry.ca.

considered full "persons" under the laws of Canada and had the freedom to purchase land, travel, and make legal arrangements. While the Wendake-Nionwentsïo, Algonquin/Missisaugas, and Anishinabewaki go through long, slow legal processes to achieve recognition of the rights taken from them, my ancestors lived in relative peace, and their home still stands. They remain the namesake for a lonely little intersection in southern Ontario. Canada is a strange place—a place where rights to land were so easily given away to settlers and are so hard-won today by people who have lived on these lands since time immemorial.

Before returning to Coast Salish territory, I want to explore the origins of my earliest ancestors and the places they first encountered when they landed on Turtle Island.

Part 2.
Way Back: 1640–1800s

8. Epekwitk (PEI): Its Original Inhabitants

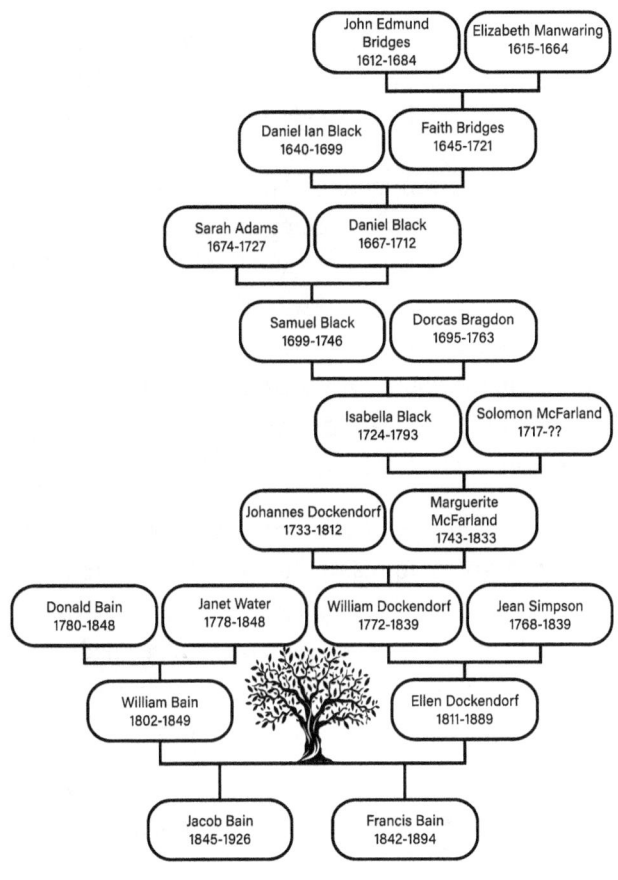

Bain Family Tree.

Temporarily leaving aside the Jelly-Foote branches of the family, in this section we'll turn to the Bain-Barker side of the family.

My first Bain ancestor settled on an island on the eastern side of Turtle Island. For thousands of years, the Mi'kmaq called the place "Epekwitk" (or "Abegweit"), meaning "resting on the waves."[60] Epekwitk has an area of approximately 5,600 square kilometres. For those of us on the western edge of Turtle Island, that means that you could fit five Epekwitk-sized islands into one Vancouver Island.

So where does the current name, Prince Edward Island, come from? British colonization led to the naming of Prince Edward Island (PEI) after Prince Edward, Duke of Kent and father of Queen Victoria. He never visited the island; the name was assigned in 1799 by the second governor of the province, after Britain granted approval. As the Mi'kmaq confederacy puts it, "The arbitrary renaming of Epekwitk ... the name the Mi'kmaq used for this Island for thousands of years, shows the colonialist attitude of the time."[61]

Before colonization, Epekwitk's population is estimated to have been about 300 Mi'kmaq residents. The Mi'kmaq did not govern their connection to land via surveying posts, lines on a map, or small pieces of paper with writing on them. They hadn't carved up Epekwitk into a grid of rectangles with sharp corners, each to be used by a different person. The Mi'kmaq political system recognized

---

[60] http://www.gov.pe.ca/infopei/index.php3?number=19670&lang=E Out of respect for Mi'kmaq territory, I've used Epekwitk for the place often called Prince Edward Island (PEI). I've continued to use PEI, though, when directly referencing documents regarding the colonial/provincial administration.

[61] For a brief summary, see the CBC "How Prince Edward, who never set foot on PEI ended up with an Island named after him." https://www.cbc.ca/news/canada/prince-edward-island/pei-prince-edward-250-1.4382116.

Epekwitk as one of the seven political districts of the Mi'kmaq of the Atlantic Region. These districts, which included the Gaspé Peninsula and parts of Maine, made up the Mi'kmaq Nation under the leadership of the Mi'kmaq Grand Council.[62]

The first visits of European explorers and colonizers to Epekwitk took place from 1534, the year of Jacques Cartier's first voyage, to the early 1700s. In the 1720s, the first French settler-colonists established homes at Port La Joie and St. Peters. They called the island Ile St-Jean, and they aimed to make it a granary for their fort at Louisbourg, Cape Breton. In the early 1700s, with only a few hundred French residents, the French and Mi'kmaq populations were likely approximately equivalent. During this time, the French engaged with the Mi'kmaq for the most part as allies, on a nation-to-nation basis. Annual celebrations included the exchange of presents celebrating their alliance.[63]

After the fall of Louisbourg, Acadian (French-descendent) settlers were expelled from the Bay of Fundy in neighbouring Nova Scotia. Many Acadians came to Epekwitk as refugees; there are oral stories and documents that record the interactions between these cultures.[64] The Acadians were then deported from Epekwitk as well, leaving a small population of 300 Acadians and an unrecorded number of Mi'kmaq residents when the island was surrendered to the British in 1763.

---

[62] First Residents and the Arrival of Europeans, https://www.princeedwardisland.ca/en/information/executive-council-office/first-residents-and-arrival-europeans.
[63] Tammy MacDonald, Research Director, Mi'kmaq Confederacy of PEI. Mi'kmaq Presence on Prince Edward Island: a 12,000 year history http://mcpei.ca/wp-content/uploads/2019/04/Mikmaq-History-on-PEI-Apr-2019.pdf
[64] ibid.

In 1764, a British surveyor divided the land into 67 large "townships," 20,000 acres each, which were allocated in a lottery to military officers and well-connected residents of Britain, many of whom never even visited PEI. Each parcel of land was given under the condition that they settle the land with at least 100 Protestant "tenants." That would mean an aspirational total of at least 6,700 settlers within a decade.

As the lands were settled, the pattern of absentee land ownership and preference for Protestant residents persisted. Up until the early 1800s, immigration to the colony was primarily from the Scottish Highlands.[65] Some came in larger groups—for example, Lord Selkirk, Thomas Douglas, in 1803 brought a group of 800 Scottish Highlanders to PEI. A government report suggests that in the mid-1800s, approximately half of the PEI population was Scottish, making it the most Scottish province or state on Turtle Island.[66] Many of the migrants spoke primarily Scottish Gaelic. A report from 1843 states that, in seeking a minister, "They wish to secure the labours of one who can preach in both English and Gaelic, which appears to be necessary as there are so many in that section that speak the Gaelic."[67]

---

[65] http://www.gov.pe.ca/photos/original/population_bkg.pdf: Although proprietors were obliged to settle their properties with "foreign Protestants," a great deal of the subsequent immigration into the colony was undirected. Moreover, it was never "foreign" and only sometimes "Protestant." Highland Scots dominated the early British colonization period.

[66] Government of PEI Historical Milestones, http://www.gov.pe.ca/infopei/index.php3?number=12183&lang=E.

[67] http://www.islandnewspapers.ca/islandora/object/guardian%3A19370925-010 "History of the North River Baptist Church" By Gordon C. Warren, of Acadia University, Wolfville, N.S. a Native Son – Sept 1932.

Let's pause for a moment to sum up these events. Mi'kmaq had been residents on the land for thousands of years. In the 1700s, they were sharing the land with French-speaking peoples and celebrating their ongoing allyship. Then, in 1764, the new English ruler decided to subdivide the entire land of Epekwitk and literally give away every inch of the Island in a land lottery, without leaving even a corner for the Mi'kmaq! And in another twist, since the land had been given away entirely into private hands, even the PEI colonial government had control over very little land.

Thus by the early 1800s, as immigration sharply increased, the Mi'kmaq were increasingly marginalized when it came to their access to land. They moved from the main island of PEI to smaller islands just off the coast, such as Lennox Island, which had not been allocated through the British lottery.

Mi'kmaq leaders spoke out about their maltreatment at the hands of colonial rulers. In 1808, "Indians, inhabitants of Lennox Island" petitioned the PEI government, requesting recognition of their land and rights to the territory, and that the Island be purchased rather than merely taken. In the 1840s, Chief Thomas Labone of the "Micmac Tribe of Indians" sent a letter to the Crown mentioning their better relationship with the French with regards to land.

> *In former times our Fathers were the Owners of this Island and fully Enjoyed the Resources thereof until they were visited by the People of the French after which by a Treaty entered into that Nation with Your Majesty's Government, our People became British Subjects; since which our Tribe has been deprived of their Hunting Grounds without receiving any Remuneration for the Loss they sustained by*

> which Privation and Want have reduced our once numerous Tribe in this Island to a Skeleton of Five Hundred Individuals ..."[68]

Non-Mi'kmaq residents of Epekwitk also wrote to their government about the abject poverty of the "Indians." One such letter, from Charles Augustus FitzRoy, Governor of PEI at the time, stated that "their [the Mi'kmaq] numbers are rapidly decreasing and, with few exceptions, they are sunk to the most abject and degraded state to which I should conceive it possible for human beings to arrive."[69]

The government approached various landowners to purchase land, but by the 1860s the Mi'kmaq still had "no land to call their own."[70] The Indian Commissioner ended up being a resourceful advocate for the Mi'kmaq:

> In the 1800s, Indian Commissioner Theophilus Stewart urged the PEI government to provide for more land, a place for "Indians who have no land to call their own," but received only negative replies. In desperation, Stewart approached the Aborigines Protection Society in London, England, to purchase Lennox Island for the Mi'kmaq. Struck with the idea, the Society immediately began a subscription campaign to raise money to purchase the island. It was eventually purchased in 1870 for £400 and was held by the Society for the "use of the Aboriginal Population of Prince Edward Island." The title to

---

[68] Mi'kmaq History on PEI, Mi'kmaq Confederacy of PEI. http://mcpei.ca/wp-content/uploads/2019/04/Mikmaq-History-on-PEI-Apr-2019.pdf.
[69] ibid, p. 3.
[70] Tammy MacDonald, Research Director, MCPEI. Creation of the Reserves on PEI. http://www.mcpei.ca/files/u1/Creation_of_the_Reserves_on_PEI_1.pdf.

the land was to be held by a board of trustees, one of whom was PEI Indian Commissioner Theophilus Stewart.[71]

While this solution did provide access to land, the land was not owned and controlled by Mi'kmaq, but rather by a separate Society and board of trustees.

There were three other small pieces of land at least temporarily allocated for Mi'kmaq:

> *Other land, in Lots 15 and 55, was purchased for the Mi'kmaq in 1852. On Lot 55, the land was poor, and subsequently, was not used by the Mi'kmaq. Lot 15's land was very good, and was quickly taken over by "white, Irish squatters." 10 acres of Ordnance Land was loaned by the War Department for the use of eleven Mi'kmaq families. This "Ordnance Reserve" was used extensively, with the resident Mi'kmaq families building a road and planting fields of potatoes.*[72]

The "Ordnance Reserve" mentioned above, on the eastern shore of Charlottetown Harbour, would have been the closest official Mi'kmaq settlement to the Bain farm (mentioned below). However, even this land allocation was short-lived, as noted in 1866:

---

[71] "By 1912, the trustees for Lennox Island had either died or were very elderly. The land reverted to the Crown (King George V) and became known as an 'Ordinary Reserve.'" Taken from *Stories from our Elders: Stories and Teachings from an Atlantic Circle of Knowledge Keepers* https://www.apcfnc.ca/images/uploads/Download_Book.pdf, Sept 16 2018.

[72] Tammy MacDonald, Research Director, MCPEI. Creation of the Reserves on PEI. http://www.mcpei.ca/files/u1/Creation_of_the_Reserves_on_PEI_1.pdf.

> *The "Ordnance Reserve" land was seized by the government of PEI and a Fever Hospital was placed upon the exact 10 acres used by the Mi'kmaq.* [73]

During the latter part of the 19th century, Mi'kmaq lived for the most part in "informal settlements" on private parcels of land across the island. Much later, in 1912, a local Mi'kmaq resident claimed continuous occupancy on Rocky Point, just south of the Bains' property and Charlottetown. This fourth and last reserve was a tiny three acres. Through their struggles for land and recognition, rough estimates indicate that the Mi'kmaq maintained a total population of approximately 250 to 300.[74]

Let's now return to the story of my ancestors as they stepped foot on Epekwitk for the first time.

---

[73] Ibid.
[74] http://www.mcpei.ca/files/u1/Mi_kmaq_history_on_PEI_1.pdf.

9. "The First Bain": William Bain of Epekwitk, 1760s-1890s

William Bain	Ellen Dockendorff
1802-1849	1811-1889
Jacob Bain	Charlotte Simpson
1845-1926	1842-1905
William Simpson Bain	Kathleen E. Griffiths
1886-1962	1893-1967
Ian Bain	Claudia Ada Barker
1919-1995	1917-2018

William Bain was the first in my paternal ancestral line to arrive in Canada. His and my last name, Bain, is mostly likely derived from Scottish Gaelic bàn, meaning "white," "fair." In Gaelic, the name would be Bàin (masculine), and Bhàin (feminine).

In case you didn't catch that: my Bain ancestors were settlers from Great Britain, with a last name that means "white"!

William Bain was born in Thurso, Caithness, Scotland, in 1802, the second of six siblings. Thurso is, in fact, the northernmost town on the British mainland, at approximately the same latitude as Juneau, Alaska. Thurso is close enough to Norway that it became a significant port city during the Norse occupation—which ended in 1266.

Thurso was and still is a small town; in 1831, when my ancestors lived there, the population was around 4,500.[75] Even with today's roads and vehicles, Google suggests that a drive from Glasgow to Thurso would take approximately five hours—two hours beyond the nearest city, Inverness.

By the early 19th century, the second wave of what was called the "Highland Clearances" was underway. Landlords in the Highlands, including the area around Thurso, evicted small-scale farmers from their property and "enclosed" shared lands. As a result of these expulsions, there was an increasing population of highland Scots on the coast and emigrating out of Scotland.

Newspapers in Scotland in the 1820s and 1830s were full of headlines about various parts of Canada. The Inverness Journal of 1821 published the notice: "Nova Scotia – Notice with Inverness agents of land for sale in Nova Scotia." An article of 1822 announced "Nova Scotia & the neighbouring Islands of Canada – MacDonald & Elder, Sleat, Isle of Skye, intend to fit out transports for the conveyance of passengers from Inverness & the West Coast." The service was particularly extended to Highlanders: "Robert Hunter, Greenock, advertising fast-sailing coppered ships to go in June next to any port on island in the North Highlands where emigrants wish to embark." Canada was the place to go and start a new life.

So a stonemason named William Bain, aged 27, got a ticket aboard the brig Matilda from Cork, likely with his parents, Donald and Janet. They arrived in Saint John, New Brunswick, in 1834: a bustling city

---

[75] And things haven't changed much: as of 2011 it was still only 8,000 people. https://familysearch.org/learn/wiki/en/Thurso,_Caithness,_Scotland. More info: http://www.scottishaccommodationindex.com/thursopics.htm.

with a population of 20,000 people, up from 12,000 just 10 years earlier. They made their way to Charlottetown, PEI, at that point a separate colony of England.

William was a stonemason, and an enterprising sort—or at least enterprising enough to compose and post an advertisement in the local paper:

> *Plain and Ornamental Stone Cutting*
>
> *The Subscriber respectfully tenders his grateful acknowledgements to the Inhabitants of Charlottetown, and the Island at large, for the favours he has received since he commenced business, and begs leave to inform them that he is now carrying on the above business in Water Street, opposite Mr. John Gainsford's brick house, where an extensive assortment of the very best quality of Head Stones, Tomb Stones, Hearth Stones, Grinding Stones, Stove pipe Stones, Jamb Stones, and all descriptions of House-building stones, are furnished and executed punctually, in the neatest manner, and on the most reasonable terms ... From several years' constant practice in several of the principal towns in Great Britain, the Subscriber feels confident that he will give satisfaction to those who may favour him with their commands.*
>
> *William Bain*
>
> *Charlottetown, Dec. 28, 1834*[76]

His work subsequent to this notice must have been satisfactory, because just under ten years later William was a stone cutter for the

---

[76] Island Narratives Project, William, Francis and Laura Bain: http://vre2.upei.ca/cap/node/887.

building of the Colonial House in Charlottetown.[77] While the building was paid for by the British government, the labour and materials to construct it were primarily local. As the PEI government reports:

> *When tenders for trades were accepted, it was found necessary to leave the Island only for stone, which was brought from Nova Scotia. Stone-masonry, brick-laying, carpentry, joinery, plastering, slating, painting, glazing, sheet metal working and excavating were all done by Islanders, proud that the new Colonial Building was indeed a local accomplishment ...*[78]

What was then called the Colonial Building has now become Province House in downtown Charlottetown: the provincial legislature and the site where the documents of Canadian Confederation were signed in 1867.[79]

William Bain warranted a brief biography, published in a local church history, in which the biographer notes, "He continued his work as a mason and builder, and in association with a Mr. Watts, he built the Provincial Government Building in Charlottetown."[80]

He was a deeply religious man, as referenced by the church he attended:

---

[77] Construction took place 1843–1847.
[78] from http://www.pc.gc.ca/eng/lhn-nhs/pe/provincehouse/natcul/natcul1.aspx.
[79] Colonial House was where the "Fathers of Confederation" met in the 1860s. The building has since been renamed "Province House," like much of Canada retaining the colonial infrastructure while changing the terminology.
[80] "History of the North River Baptist Church" By Gordon C. Warren, of Acadia University Wolfville, N.S. a Native Son – Sept 1932. http://www.islandnewspapers.ca/islandora/object/guardian%3A19370925-010.

Wm. Bain had been reared a Presbyterian and was a staunch upholder of the principles of that church until the year 1836 when he experienced a deep conviction of sin, became exercised over the question of baptism, and was finally baptized into the [Baptist] church at York and West Rivers. A deeply spiritual man, he proved a tower of strength to his church, especially in the Sabbath school and prayer meetings, and was a most generous supporter of the gospel. [81]

It's unclear how William met Ellen Dockendorff. She was more closely connected to Epekwitk than he, having been born on the island,[82] with several generations of family residing on Turtle Island. Ellen and William married in 1839 and settled in a village called North River, located in Lot 32 of Queen's County,[83] about seven kilometres outside of the capital city of Charlottetown. They soon had four children: William, Francis, Jane, and Jacob.

William Bain, married for only ten years, died at just 47, when his youngest child was four years old. Ellen raised their children and lived for 40 years after his death, matriarch of a whole new generation. She lived to see the birth of 19 of her 21 grandchildren[84] on Epekwitk.

In contrast to the somewhat constant Mi'kmaq population, during the 1800s the Bain family expanded significantly. In the direct Bain line, the eldest son of Ellen and William died before his 20th birthday. However, the other three each had a large number of children, so

---

[81] "History of the North River Baptist Church" By Gordon C. Warren, of Acadia University, Wolfville, N.S. a Native Son – Sept 1932. http://www.islandnewspapers.ca/islandora/object/guardian%3A19370925-010.

[82] Ellen's family, which is explored in further depth in section 12, had roots back to Maine.

[83] As described by the British survey of 1767.

[84] Total of nine through Francis Bain, five by Jacob Bain, and seven through Jane Drake (nee Bain).

that between 1820 and 1900, the Bain clan grew from two to 50 members, a 25-fold expansion.

The Bains were one small part of a flood of expanding settlement on Epekwitk. Over the same period, the total settler population of PEI increased significantly, from 23,000 in 1820 to more than 60,000 by 1851 and increasing five-fold to 109,000 by 1891.[85] During this same period of time, as Chief Thomas Labone put it, the Mi'kmaq were reduced to "a Skeleton of Five Hundred Individuals" or even less.

---

[85] This population is fairly close to the 2011 population of just under 150,000 residents.

10. Francis Bain and the Fossil Fern of Epekwitk, 1842–1894

The Bain family became best known in Epekwitk for the work of Francis Bain, William and Ellen's second-eldest son (and brother to my ancestor Jacob). He is remembered by a stone that still stands on the lawn of the legislature building, which William had helped to construct:

"Francis Bain, Naturalist. 1842–1894. Erected by the Natural History and Antiquarian Society of P.E.I." Photo: Mali Bain, 2005.

From a young age, Francis was actively involved in the PEI settler community. In 1849, at the age of seven, he experienced the death of his father. It's likely he then took on more work on the 142-acre Bain farm—the size of it much larger than the "reserve lands" set aside for the Mi'kmaq. As noted earlier, his father had been deacon at the North River Baptist Church; starting in his early 20s, Francis volunteered as church clerk, a role he kept for 25 years. It wouldn't have been the most glamourous of tasks, probably entailing responsibility for recording minutes of meetings, keeping track of services, and updating church archives.

Francis married rather late for his day, at 33. He married Caroline Matilda Clark, age 23, whom he called affectionately "my Carrie." By the time he died at the age of 52, they had had nine children and his youngest daughter, Laura, was only four years old.

Francis worked on the farm during the days and spent evenings studying and writing to the light of a gas lantern. One of his strong interests was the natural world, both plants and rocks. Despite not having completed high school,[86] he became an amateur botanist, studying the ferns and herbs of Epekwitk. He drew detailed sketches of all kinds of flowers and is credited with having written and illustrated the natural history textbooks used by PEI public school students in the late 1800s.

Francis's approach was to create collections of specimens of plants found on Epekwitk and its small neighbour, St. Peter's Island. Francis's eye for detail, along with his interest in the

---

[86] He attended school at the home of a pastor's wife until 13 or 14 years old, and then took a few terms in Charlottetown before being pulled out of school because of his brother's illness.

natural world, made him an eloquent interpreter of what he saw. Some of his descriptions said as much about the author as about nature, as is evident, for example, in this description of one of the "Winter Birds of PEI"[87]:

> *The Purple Finch frequently winters here. He does not frequent the abodes of men, but the lonely forest, where the domed summits of the great yellow birches, Betula excels, are thick-laden with strobiles, is his home. The stay-at-homes never see him. But on a keen, bright morning, when the gilded twigs are surging aloft in the frigid blue, from their loftiest tops rings out the glad, sweet carol to startle and charm the adventurous woodman.*

Francis was indeed an adventurous woodman: he undertook what he described as "expeditions to farflung corners of the Island." Those expeditions would have been by train or by horse and wagon; sometimes he brought his wife Carrie or son Waldo (Waddie).

Starting in 1881 and for 11 years, Francis wrote a regular column appearing in the Daily Examiner, sharing observations of birds, wildlife, weather, flowers, geology, and his various travels. His columns conveyed his great appreciation for the natural beauty of Epekwitk. Here is one from 1885, describing the climate:

> Sheltered from the chilling breath of the Labrador Current by the primary ridges of Nova Scotia and Cape Breton, it enjoys a summer season with a more elevated temperature, a purer atmosphere, a clearer sky, and more abounding sunshine on its rich, verdure-clad swells, than are to be found on the immediate Atlantic seaboard. In

---

[87] The *Canadian Science Monthly* 3(9) Sept 1885 127-129. Retrieved from http://eco.canadiana.ca/view/oocihm.8_04165_17/10?r=0&s=1.

> winter, on the contrary ... snow lies deep on the ground, and the rivers and bays for four months are firmly locked in ice. The atmosphere, however, is pure and bracing, and free from the damp chilling mists of the ocean seaboard.[88]

He was an active member of the Natural History and Antiquarian Society. In addition to botanical interests, Francis had a strong interest in many fields of natural history. Again working as an amateur, he explored local geology and, made the estimation that Epekwitk had been connected to the mainland 3,000 years ago. Contemporary scientists bear out his belief, though they put the number at approximately 5,000 years ago.

Francis's interest in natural science was shared by others in the mid- to late 1800s. Natural history societies were some of the first organizations in Canada to focus on intellectual activities. They purchased books, collected specimens (botanical or geological), and organized lectures. In Victorian times it was fashionable for "people of culture" to follow intellectual pursuits in their leisure time; natural science was "immensely satisfying to the Victorian psyche, for it comfortably amalgamated religious, scientific, and aesthetic sensibilities."[89]

Francis was highly respected by his peers for what he was able to accomplish despite his isolation:

> Without the advantages of a liberal education and largely self-taught, handicapped in this insular Province by isolation from the fellowship

---

[88] Ibid.
[89] "Prince Edward Island's Early Natural History Society" by Winifred (Cairns) Wake http://vre2.upei.ca/islandmagazine/fedora/repository/vre:islemag-batch2-496/OBJ/07_Prince_Edward_Island-s_early_Natural_p_27-33.pdf. p. 27.

and the stimulation that come from fellow scientists and learned societies ... he, nevertheless, became, through tireless perseverance, while supporting a family by toiling on his farm, and remains to this hour, the foremost naturalist that his native Province has produced.[90]

Francis was considered by his eulogizer a "patriot":

He loved his native land, its birds and plants and even its very stones to him were dear. Our boys and girls we hope will be inspired the more they know of their native land to love it more, for how can they love another land so well. There is need for more patriotism and more knowledge of our own land and its resources.[91]

I find it fascinating to hear the assumptions revealed in the voices of his contemporaries. The references to "our own land" and "patriotism" demonstrate the confidence with which residents of Epekwitk assumed the validity and value of the 1764 land lottery, which had created so many challenges.

Francis was born on Epetwik and grew to greatly respect and appreciate the stones, plants, and birds of the land. In these journeys, he would probably have had encounters with the Mi'kmaq, who had been living on that land for thousands of years. Did he meet Mi'kmaq residents and learn from them the ways that they observed, recorded, and made use of these plants and animals?

We have no record of Francis's interactions, or lack of them, with the Mi'kmaq; in all of the accounts that remain, I could not find a mention of Indigenous plant names, uses, or culture. Despite the lack of records, I wonder if, in his "adventurous" excursions, when he

---

[90]   http://www.islandnewspapers.ca/islandora/object/guardian%3A19370925-010.
[91]   Eulogy of Francis Bain, 1905.

encountered a Mi'kmaq group, he might have exchanged pleasantries and a bit more, in mutual appreciation of the beauty of Epekwitk.

Around the same time that Francis Bain was gaining accolades for his amateur scientific work, an Irish immigrant, Thomas Irwin, had come to learn and develop appreciation for the beauty and complexity of the Mi'qmaw language. He wrote elementary schoolbooks in Mi'qmaw and spent 13 years attempting to persuade the PEI government to share the cost of publishing them. However, his efforts were unsuccessful; as one summary put it: "the majority of members agreed that the Indians should be instructed, if at all, in English, and there was no point in preserving their 'barren language' from its inevitable extinction."[92] Though Irwin had written both a grammar and a schoolbook in Mi'qmaw, neither were used either in PEI or in Nova Scotia.

Even if Francis had attempted to document or learn from Mi'kmaq approaches, the scientific community, like the educational community, was not particularly welcoming of new approaches to taxonomy or nomenclature. Francis did attempt to identify and name some "new" species in Epekwitk, primarily through his ornithological book Birds of PEI.[93] Although he named a whole range of birds, even his standard-sounding names did not conform to the dominant (European/American) naming protocols. Quotes from reviewers are illustrative:

---

[92] L.F.S. Upton. *Indians and Islanders: the Micmacs in Colonial Prince Edward Island*, p. 28.
[93] An archived online copy of this book can be found at https://archive.org/details/birdsofprinceedwoobain/page/n9.

> We regret much that Mr. Bain did not adopt some more modern nomenclature for his birds ... it is well to conform, for the present, to the view of great American scientists until the more conservative voices of Canadian naturalists can have greater power.
>
> At a future time we hope to see Mr. Bain, who is an enthusiastic naturalist, undertake a revised list, in which further particulars and greater preciseness will be found. He has been working alone in his locality, and therefore he deserves sincere thanks of orthinologists [sic] for what he has already done.[94]

Despite facing critique from the "centre" of scientific and botanical knowledge, Francis was universally recognized and respected as the foremost amateur naturalist of PEI. His contribution was recognized not only by the stone mentioned earlier, but also in a rather more unusual way. In his wanderings and adventures, Francis Bain discovered a fossil fern that was "new to science." Sir William Dawson, a Canadian geologist,[95] named it Tylodendron Baini after Francis Bain. Thus, when it came time to name one of the oldest ferns in Epekwitk, it was one of the newcomers to the island who was honoured, not the ancient caretakers of this land.

---

[94] http://eco.canadiana.ca/view/oocihm.8_04952_370/8?r=0&s=1.
[95] Mentioned at the end of this article: http://www.islandnewspapers.ca/islandora/object/guardian%3A19370925-010. "History of the North River Baptist Church" By Gordon C. Warren, of Acadia University, Wolfville, N.S. Sept 1932.

11. Wabanaki Confederacy and Pemaquid

The earliest branches of the Bain-Dockendorff family settled south of Epekwitk, in what is now known as the US state of Maine, in the early 1700s. Land was at the heart of conflicts among British, French, and Indigenous nations in the "Indian Wars" of the 1700s and beyond. Indigenous leaders faced a complex series of choices during these years. As settlers continued to pour into their lands, they made strategic choices to resist colonial impositions, assert sovereignty, and cooperate with settlers as allies and trading partners. As Victoria Freeman puts it:

> *Individual native leaders were able to maintain their own power and hold on to their followers only if they were able to protect their people and their interests and were perceived as coping effectively with the various threats posed by English colonization ...* [96]

Several nations on the eastern side of Turtle Island had combined forces to form the Wabanaki Confederacy, a multinational agreement that included the Abenaki tribal communities, Maliseet Passamaquoddy and later also the Mi'kmaq. The term Abenaki or Wabanaki is sometimes translated as "People of the Dawnland." It is based on waban ("light" or "white," referring to the dawn in the east), and aki ("land"). The Mi'kmaq referred to the Wabanaki

---

[96] Freeman, Victoria. Distant Relations: How My Ancestors Colonized North America. p. 173.

Confederacy as their "Convention Council," calling it Buduswagan, based on the word putu, meaning "orator."[97]

In 1721, the Wabanaki Confederacy presented the English with a formal letter:

> Thou seest from the peace treaty of which I am sending the copy that thou must live peacefully with me. Is it living peacefully with me to take my land away from me against my will? My land which I received from God alone, my land of which no king nor foreign power has been allowed, or is allowed to dispose against my will, which thou hast been doing none the less for several years, by establishing and fortifying thyself here against my wishes. ... Consider, great captain that I have often told thee to withdraw from my land and that I am telling thee so again for the last time. My land is not thine either by right or conquest, or by grant or by purchase.[98]

The ensuing war was called the 4th Wabanaki-New English War of 1722–1725, or at times, Dummer's War (1723–1726) after the (opportune, perhaps) name of the then-governor of Massachusetts. During the war, Wabanaki Confederacy fighters raided eastern New England, and English troops massacred entire villages at Norridgewock and in the Penobscot Valley.

The conflict ended with a series of meetings on the Maine coast, in Boston, and in the Confederacy. These were multilingual and

---

[97] Prins, Harald E.L. "Storm Clouds Over Wabanaki Confederacy Diplomacy Until Dummer's Treaty (1727)" Written for the Atlantic Policy Congress of First Nations Chiefs, Amherst, Nova Scotia, Canada. As accessed at https://www.wabanaki.com/wabanaki_new/The_Wabanaki.html.
[98] ibid.

multinational meetings, which would have required significant translation and interpretation throughout.

The Penobscot orator, Loron Sagouarrab, as well as other Wabanaki leaders, negotiated for the Confederacy. After several rounds of negotiations and travel throughout the area, Governor Dummer drafted a treaty text for the Confederacy to take back and consider. When Sagouarrab was read the draft of the "Dummer's Treaty," he wrote a clear and angry response:

> *The disagreement between your writings & what I spoke to you viva voce [in actual speech] stops me & makes me suspend my negotiation till I have receiv'd your answer. I thought to have spoken justly and according to the interests of my nation, but I have had the confusion to see that my words have been taken in a quite contrary sense ...*
>
> *As for what relates to your King, when you have ask'd me if I acknowledged him for king I answer'd yes but at the same time have made you take notice that I did not understand to acknowledge him for my king butt only that I own'd that he was king in his kingdom as the king of France is king in his.*[99]

It is powerful to read these words from a Wabanaki orator: I can almost hear his frustration, and the frustration of generations of Indigenous peoples whose conversations and relationships with colonial powers were translated into legal language that attempted to undermine their sovereignty. Having these words recorded shines light on some of the hidden dynamics behind the legalese of treaties written by the British.

---

[99] ibid.

The Confederacy, including representatives of Abenaki, Maliseet, and Mi'kmaq nations, met at St. Francis (Obenak) near Montreal, and eventually agreed to both strengthen the cross-border Wabanaki Confederacy and to sign the treaty.

Later, when signing the treaties, Sagouarrab again referred to conversations he had with Dummer:

> *I say, he never said to me—Give thyself and thy land to me, nor acknowledge my King for thy King, as thy ancestors formerly did. He again said to me—But do you not recognize the King of England as King over all his states? To which I answered—Yes, I recognize him King over all his lands; but I rejoined, do not hence infer that I acknowledge thy King as my King, and King of my lands. Here is my distinction—my Indian distinction. God hath willed that I have no King, and that I be master of my lands in common.*
>
> *What I tell you now is the truth. If, then, any one should produce any writing that makes me speak otherwise, pay no attention to it, for I know not what I am made to say in another language, but I know well what I say in my own.*[100]

This powerful statement rings true for Sagouarrab and, I would guess, for many generations of Indigenous translators and negotiators across Turtle Island.

My ancestors lived at Bristol, then known as Pemaquid, in today's Maine, one of the earliest British settlements on the eastern coast of what is now the United States. The area had been ruled by a Bashaba,

---

[100] Prins, Harald E.L. "Storm Clouds over Wabanaki Confederacy Diplomacy Until Drummer's Treaty (1727)". Invited article written for the Atlantic Policy Congress of First Nations Chiefs, Amherst, Nova Scotia, Canada.

or Great Ruler, by the name of Mavooshen, and his chief residence was said to be Pemaquid, meaning "long point."

The first British fort at Pemaquid, built in 1625, was a year-round trading post for the fur trade, providing protection from sea pirates. Some of those pirates, such as Dixie Bull and Captain Kidd, are now part of folk history; however, at the time the danger of attack was very real and serious. In fact, in 1632 Pemaquid was raided by Dixie Bull, and in 1689, just a few decades before my ancestor Isabella Black was born there, all the inhabitants of Pemaquid were either killed or taken prisoner by French attackers.

Pemaquid, like many other forts of its time, was built for the exclusive use and protection of settlers even prior to the "Indian Wars" of the 1700s. A stone inscription at Pemaquid, set up in 1908, recalls this history:

> Commemorative to the Early European Settlement in this Locality which was the Resort of the White Men from the Earliest Period of the History of New England ...

Amid pirate attacks and conflicts between colonial powers, references to conflict with Indigenous peoples were a consistent theme in European perceptions of the "New World" of the time. A note written by the Earl of Egmont in the 1700s describes the colonies as:

> a small people, forming or formed into a small society in the vast, impervious, and dangerous forests of America, intersected with seas, bays, lakes, rivers, marshes, and mountains; without roads, without inns or accommodations, locked up for half the year by snow and intense frost, and where the settler can scarce straggle from his

> habitation five hundred yards, even in times of peace, without risk of being intercepted, scalped, and murdered.[101]

While these narratives may sound extreme, the conflict between nations at the time was real and violent.

Colonel David Dunbar rebuilt and renamed Pemaquid as Fort Frederic in 1729–30. He laid out a plan for the territory, assigned British names—Townshend, Harrington, Walpole—and began inviting settlers to reside there. As a later writer put it, "the greatest mistake the Colonel made, was in not giving the settlers who held their possessions under him, clear titles to their lands; they received from him neither deeds nor leases."[102]

While encouraged by the British governor at the time, the settlements of the early 1700s were not supported by any land title or treaty.

---

[101] Quoted in Duncan Campbell, History of Prince Edward Island, http://www.gutenberg.org/files/35835/35835-h/35835-h.htm#chapter-i.
[102] *Trail of the Maine Pioneer*, Maine Federation of Women's Clubs, 1916.

12. New England Settlers, 1635–1740s

John Edmund Bridges 1612–1685	Elizabeth Manwaring 1615–1664
Faith Bridges 1645–1721	Daniel Ian Black 1640–1699
Daniel Black 1677–1712	Sarah Adams 1674–1727
Samuel Black 1699–1746	Dorcas Bragdon 1695–1764
Isabella Black 1724–1793	Solomon McFarland 1717–??
Margeurite McFarland 1743–1833	Johannes Dockendorff 1733–1812
William Dockendorff 1772–1839	Jean Simpson 1768–1839
Ellen Dockendorff 1811–1889	William Bain 1802–1849
Jacob Bain 1845–1926	Charlotte Simpson 1842–1905
William Simpson Bain 1886–1962	Kathleen E. Griffiths 1893–1967
Ian Bain 1919–1995	Claudia Ada Barker 1917–2018

My grandmother and I, bent over the table, studied a painstakingly typed family tree: the Bains, back five generations, to PEI and beyond. Near the top of the tree: William Bain.

Beside him, his wife: Ellen Dockendorff.

"Who was that, Grandma?"

"I don't know much about her. She was a German lady," my grandma responded.

"Grandma, I didn't know we had German ancestry!"

"Well, she married a Scottish man."

"She's still German!"

"Well, depends on how you look at it, then," she said, with her typical dry wit.

In fact, Ellen Dockendorff was born on PEI, and her mother was from Scotland (like so many PEI residents of the time). She did have a German grandfather; thus, the name Dockendorff. However, it was her maternal ancestors that caught my eye. A full seven generations before Ellen, there was her great-great-great-great-great grandfather, John Edmund Bridges. In 1635, John, a 23-year-old blacksmith from Cripplegate, London, England, boarded the James and sailed to Lynn, Essex, Massachusetts.

John Bridges' craft was integral in his new place of residence, so much so that his name is recorded in a court document a few years later: "The general court 26 May 1647 ordered him to answer at Essex Court for neglect to further public service by delaying to shoe

Mr. Symond's horse when he was about to come to court."[103] John married Elizabeth Manwaring from Shropshire, England.

Isabella Black, John Bridges's great-great-granddaughter, warrants an even longer pause. Isabella lived in Pemaquid (Bristol) well before the American Revolution and almost 100 years before William Bain immigrated.

Isabella was born in Pemaquid in 1724, to Samuel Black and Dorcas Bragdon. It was a small settlement: at the time Isabella was 12 years old, a total of 27 individuals were residing at Pemaquid. One of those was Solomon McFarland, whom Isabella married in her late teens.

There is a collection of stories about Solomon and Isabella recorded by their descendants. The first is said to have happened on July 19, 1745, soon after their marriage:

> *During an Indian raid [Isabella] was picking berries in a field a little distance from the fort, "when she saw an Indian partly concealed, scarcely a gunshot from her and she realized she should be seeking a place of safety but to run meant instant death, so she stepped slowly away for some distance then began to run for her life. The Indian fired and she fell, the bullet merely grazing her shoulder, producing a slight wound, but she was now within range of the fort guns and the guards being aroused by the report of the Indian's piece, the Indian sought safety in flight."*[104]

A few years later, in 1747, Solomon and his sons Walter and George were attacked by Indigenous fighters while on John's Island. George

---

[103] *The Pioneers of Massachusetts, 1620–1650* p. 67.
[104] From *Ancestors of James Wilson Yates*, pp. 59–60. Hitchcock Publisher, New York: 1926.

was killed, Solomon escaped, and Walter was held in captivity for two years, long enough to learn Indigenous languages. Apparently, at the Indian Conference at Falmouth in 1749, his father recognized him only by his voice, as his appearance and manner were completely Indigenous. It is said that after his release he became a very important interpreter.[105]

These stories of the McFarland family suggest that the family was present and very much involved in Indigenous-settler relations. Conflicts and negotiations for New England took place during the time that Isabella and Solomon were growing up, getting married, and raising their two sons and four daughters.

Did they see themselves as visitors/settlers on Indigenous land, or as rightful colonial possessors of the land? It is almost certain that they knew and connected with Indigenous peoples as part of their daily life. It is less clear how directly they connected with members of the Wabanaki Confederacy, and whether Walter McFarland might have interpreted for orators such as Loron Sagourrab.

---

[105] Paraphrased from *A History of Bristol and Bremen*, 1972.

13. Lenape and Susquehannock of the Delaware River

About 800 kilometres south of the McFarlands, on the Delaware River near present-day Philadelphia, lived another early set of ancestors.

The Delaware River is the home of the Lenape, also known as the Lenni-Lenape or the Delaware Indians. The Lenape are an Algonquin-speaking nation; the name Lenape means "Men of Men" or "Original People."[106] The Lenape had a semi-nomadic maize harvesting tradition prior to contact with settlers, and traded maize to the new settlers.

Some of my earliest ancestors immigrated to a colony on the lower reaches of the Delaware known as New Sweden. New Sweden was set up by the Swedish government at a time when Sweden was a significant international power.[107] Unlike many Turtle Island colonies, the New Sweden Colony did not enjoy consistent and regular shipments of supplies from the "Old World": instead, they were sent with significant agricultural supplies and expected to provide for their own sustenance. This made relationships with their neighbours particularly important to the survival of New Sweden. The colony consisted mostly of Swedish residents and others known as "forest Finns": Finnish residents who had been living in Sweden.[108]

---

[106] Our History" section of Nanticoke Lenni-Lenape Tribal Nation. https://nlltribe.com/our-history/.
[107] Sweden had been fairly successful in the 30 Years' War and actually occupied parts of Saxony, the German region south of Berlin.
[108] Some suggest that these early Finnish settlers were responsible for introducing the "log house" construction that has become a part of Turtle Island culture.

The Swedish government aimed to set up a colony in the New World similar to New Amsterdam (now New York), which had been established by the Dutch. The Dutch-Swedish competition was quite explicit: the founder of the colony, Peter Minuit, had been given secret instructions to situate the New Sweden colony in a location that would disrupt Dutch access to the Susquehannock fur trade in the interior. Thus, the New Swedish settlements were strategically located at a place where Indigenous and colonial trade networks overlapped.

While overt conflict between New Sweden and the Lenni-Lenape was avoided, and settler accounts suggest a primarily peaceful relationship, the peace was tense at best. According to Lenape histories, the Lenape population was being decimated by diseases from European immigrants.

Up the river from New Sweden were the Susquehannock, an Iroquois-speaking nation. They were known as "the great traders" of the interior, and estimates of their population in the 1600s range upwards of several thousand, clustered in towns of several hundred people.[109] They played a strong role in the inland trade further north with members of the Iroquois League, though they had resisted joining that confederacy. When European trade goods emerged, they travelled through the Susquehannock trade networks. The Susquehannock became powerful brokers in the fur trade, travelling into the interior in search of furs.

---

[109] Based on an estimate of "near 600 able men" for a single town, multiplied across a total of six towns. From *Early Indian History on the Susquehanna* by Abraham L. Guss, p. 17.

The area was so well established as a trading centre that a local trade jargon had developed between the Dutch and local nations. This language is seen as an example of a pidgin based on a local Indigenous language rather than on the language of the Europeans, representing again the dominant cultural influence of Indigenous peoples at the time.[110]

The Swedes and Susquehannock became partners, bridging the trade gap between Indigenous fur traders and English and Dutch purchasers. As part of their partnership, the Swedes supplied plentiful weapons to the Susquehannock, along with training in their use. In 1642, when Maryland declared war on the Susquehannock, the Swedish colonists partnered with the Susquehannock to defeat the English.

However, European settlement in the valley was contested and not always welcomed by Indigenous nations. In 1631, just before New Sweden was established, the Lenape and Susqehannock had attacked a plantation set up by the English, killing all 32 members. Perhaps to prevent a similar fate, when New Sweden was established, the first governor of the new Swedish colony signed "papers" with sachems (leaders) of the Lenape and Susquehannock peoples.

---

[110] The language was used until the takeover of the lands by the English, at which point the pidgin used became one based on English. *New Sweden in America* by Carol Hoffecker, p. 15.

14. 'We Ye Ancient Swedes': Peter Rambo and Brita Mattsdotter, 1640–1680s

Peter Gunnarson Rambo 1611–1698	Brita Mattsdotter 1630–1693
Catherine Rambo 1655–1722	Peter Mattson 1647–1699
Britta Mattson Cook 1674–1750	John Hendrickson 1666–1745
Maria Hendrickson 1662–1727	Charles Carl Springer 1658–1738
John B Springer 1698–1772	Mary Dempsey 1711–1795
David Springer 1732–1777	Margaret Oliver 1735–1820
Daniel Springer 1764–1826	Ruth Fairchild 1758–1856
Mary Springer 1802–1885	George Ashwell 1787–1856
George Ashwell 1831–1900	Rachel Sharpe 1843–1916
Bertha Mabel Ashwell 1882–1971	Charles Stanley Barker 1886–1969
Claudia Ada Barker 1917–2018	Ian Bain 1919–1995

The connection with Lenape and Susquehannock land comes from the Barker side of my family: the lineage of my grandmother, Claudia Ada Bain (née Barker). Given my grandmother's strong interest in genealogy, she would have been surprised and curious to read more about her mother's side of the family. I think she might have gotten a chuckle out of the name of one of her earliest ancestors on Turtle Island, Peter Rambo.[111]

Peter Rambo was born in Gothenburg, Sweden. He joined the second sailing of the Kalmar Nykel from Sweden to New Sweden, arriving in 1640[112]—just 18 years after the Mayflower brought the first Plymouth Colony settlers to Turtle Island. Brita Mattsdotter, his wife, may have arrived on the same ship, or on a later sailing; what is known is that Peter and Brita married in 1647. Between 1647 and 1658, Brita and Peter had five children and saw the community grow to several hundred, shrink to a low of 70 people, and then grow again to over 300 people. For their first four children, they carefully described the location of their birth as "New Sweden, Philadelphia, Pennsylvania." Their home is pictured on the next page.

---

[111] Fortunately, he was named about 300 years before the first *Rambo* movie was released, avoiding significant potential teasing.
[112] He was on the *Kalmar Nyckel*'s second voyage from Sweden to the New World in 1640. The first voyage apparently took four months!

ORIGINAL HOME OF PETER RAMBO
Near Philadelphia, Pa.

Peter Rambo house.

It seems that Peter Rambo, head of one of the first (and few) families of New Sweden, came to play a more and more significant role in the later years of the colony. As one historian put it, "he was one of the most prominent of the Swedish colonists, and was frequently honoured with high public trusts."[113] In the early days of the settlement, that meant acting as one of the deputies of the Swedish governor, John Rising.

---

[113] Smith's history of Delaware County, Pennsylvania, p. 73 as cited in A Genealogical History of the Dupuy family.

Peter Rambo was appointed to the Council in New Sweden, part of the self-governing state set up under British rule.[114] In 1674 he was made a Justice of the Peace, and then was one of the first justices to sit in the Upland Court. And finally, Peter was one of three Swedish settlers who gave legal depositions to British committees established to understand the history of the New Swedish colony. His deposition confirms his understanding that the Swedish colony had purchased land directly from the Indigenous peoples (and he further specifies that English Lord Baltimore was not involved):

> *These are to certifie whom it may concern, That we ye Ancient Swedes, planted upon the River Delaware in America, do declare, That the First of our Nation, that came & Planted in this River & the Creeks thereunto belonging, did find the Dutch possest of ye said River, and that the Lord Baltimore in those daies made no Pretentions thereunto ...*
>
> *And we do further certifie, that the Swedes did Anciently purchase of ye Natives the Lands lying from ye said Christina Creek to neer ye Falls of ye River Delaware & in Obedience to his Majestys letters Patent & his declaration together with his Royal highness's release, we have free submitted ourselves to William Penn Esq. as our Rightful Proprietary & Governor under ye Kings Majesty...*
>
> *Signed by us underwritten, who have been here about Fifty Years, on the behalf of our selves & ye rest of ye Ancient Planters, yet Living*

---

[114] Craig, Peter. "Chronology of Colonial Swedes on the Delaware 1638-1713." Originally published in Swedish Colonial News, Volume 2, Number 5 (Fall 2001) http://colonialswedes.net/History/Chronology.html. Accessed Sept 2018.

of ye Sweedish Nation, on this West side of ye River Delaware, at Wicoco ye 11th day of y month called January 1683.[115]

The latter is signed by Peter Cock, Peter Rambo, and Lasse Cock; Peter Rambo's "marck" is included as follows:

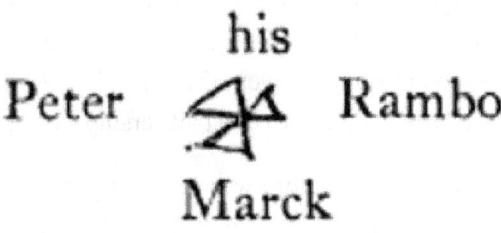

Peter Rambo's mark.

While these papers and the Swedish-Susquehannock military alliance suggest some collaboration, the leaders of New Sweden were clear that this was not their ideal arrangement. Johan Printz, Governor of New Sweden, wrote in 1644 about the Lenape: "Nothing would be better than that a couple of hundred soldiers should be sent here and kept here until we broke the necks of all of them."[116] While soldiers were not sent to destroy the Lenape, this and other quotes

---

[115] A. R. Dunlap and C.A. Weslager. "More Missing Evidence: Two Depositions by Early Swedish Settlers." The Pennsylvania Magazine of History and Biography. Vol. 91, No. 1 (January 1967), pp. 35-45.

[116] "We are Still Here: Nanticoke and Lenape History Booklet" http://nanticoke-lenape.info/images/We_Are_Still_Here_Nanticoke_and_Lenape_History_Booklet_pre-release_v2.pdf.

reveal the underlying desire of this colonial leader to exterminate their perceived opponents, the Indigenous peoples.

The Lenape and the Susquehannock strongly resisted attempts at cultural and religious assimilation by the Lutheran New Swedish colony. Governor Printz reported that "when we speak to them about God they pay no attention, but they will let it be understood that they are a free people, subject to no one, but do what they please."[117] An additional note from Printz says that "European attempts to isolate and capture Indians and convert them produced only implacable hatred. This relationship was to be a partnership, not a subjugation."[118]

In other words, a partnership was deemed possible only after an attempted subjugation. Printz's candid statements provide an insight into the mental models and understandings of the leadership of these early settlers.

In the end, the colony lasted as New Sweden for only about 20 years, and at its peak was home to no more than 600 settlers. The negotiated agreements between the New Swedish settlers and Indigenous nations were not to last: later in the 1600s, the New Sweden colony was taken over, first by the Dutch and then by the English (1664).

Given their already established trading relationships, Finnish or Swedish residents, who may have had more open-minded perspectives than their Governor, were often the "go-betweens" or mediators between the Lenape and the English.[119] The Lenape,

---

[117] "Scandinavian Colonists Confront the New World" by Karen Ordah Kupperman. In *New Sweden in North America* by Carol E. Hoffecker.
[118] Ibid.
[119] Thompson, Mark L. "New Sweden". From Encyclopedia of New Sweden. http://philadelphiaencyclopedia.org/archive/new-sweden/.

Finns, and Swedes continued their alliance throughout the 1600s, and the Lenape remained by far the most significant population in the area. As of 1670, there were only 850 Europeans and more than 3,000 Lenape in the valley.[120]

However, by the end of the 1600s, the combination of European-introduced diseases and ongoing conflict and war had reduced the Susquehannock to one village near today's Conestoga, Pennsylvania. At the same time, the numbers of settlers continued to increase exponentially.

The letter earlier quoted, signed by Peter Rambo, was a part of a series of depositions aiming to prove that Lord Baltimore had not set claim to the area of New Sweden. By 1682 the area, including New Sweden and Philadelphia, was turned over by the Crown to William Penn, the founder of Pennsylvania, and a significant influx of English Quaker settlers soon outnumbered the Swedish and Finnish settlement. Peter Rambo was considered naturalized to the new state of Pennsylvania on January 11, 1683.

To lay claim to the land, the British government sought a legal basis to legitimize its settlement. While the New Swedish colony had based their occupation of a small parcel of land on "letters" and agreements with the Lenape and Susquehannock, the British employed an empire-building approach to land acquisition throughout the colonies.

The British established a legal basis for occupation on Locke's principle of terra nullius: lands inhabited by "savages" could be considered "empty." This concept suggests a deep and basic dehumanization, as

---

[120] Sodorland, Jean. "Native Peoples to 1680". From Encyclopedia of New Sweden. http://philadelphiaencyclopedia.org/archive/native-peoples-to-1680/.

Indigenous peoples, i.e., "savages," are considered so far from human that their existence can be completely forgotten or annihilated. Since they are not considered legal persons, they cannot own land; thus, settlers can occupy the land they are on without need for further discussion.

This is a convenient principle for a settler-colonial society that aims to occupy and settle land: if the rights of Indigenous peoples do not exist, the process of land takeover is completed in the courts, without the need to declare war. The land was taken without the need to isolate, capture, or kill all the original inhabitants, as Governor Printz had once imagined.

"Old Peter Rambo," the first of my ancestors to cross the Pacific, was a member of one of the earliest colonies on Turtle Island. I don't know his personal opinions on the land he occupied, or whether he shared his governor's strong views toward Indigenous peoples. By settling and having children, he became the ancestor of hundreds, or more likely thousands, of descendants on Turtle Island. Many of those descendants, like myself, might know nothing about him. But like him, we find ourselves living and settling in places once deemed to be "empty."

15. Strathroy's "First Settler," Daniel Springer, 1780s

One of Peter Rambo's descendants, six generations later, landed in a place called Delaware, Ontario.

The township of Delaware, located between Lake Huron and Lake Erie, is located within the lands of several nations. Indigenous groups currently active in the area include the Oneida Nation of the Thames, a Haudenosaunee (Iroquois) group, and the Ojibway-Anishinaabeg of the territory of Deshkaan Ziibing (Chippewa Nation of the Thames).

Many maps from the time listed the area as Neutral. Neutral, in this case, was not a placeholder: it was the name given by the French to the people who occupied this territory. Their own name for themselves may have been Chonnonton, which means "the people who tend or manage deer." In the 1600s, the Neutral had a population of 40,000 people in about 40 settlements; they were the largest group in the area.[121] As a result of colonization, there is not currently a Neutral or Chonnonton nation or band, and there is no known record of the language they spoke or of their culture. I can feel the weight of these words, this devastating loss, in a deafening and heartbreaking silence.

Daniel Springer (1764–1826) was apparently the first white man to settle on the Thames River[122] in Ontario. He was a forerunner of what would become a quickly rising tide of settlers. Daniel was born in New York; when Daniel was barely a teenager, he and his

---

[121] Noble, William C. "The Neutral Confederacy" http://www.thecanadianencyclopedia.ca/en/article/neutral/.
[122] From the Londoner, July 18, 2013.

father fought for the British in the Revolutionary War or American War of Independence, 1775–1783. His father was killed, but Daniel survived, and was awarded 200 acres of land in Barton Township near Hamilton, Ontario.

In the 1790s he relocated to Delaware Township, where he had trading relationships with Indigenous residents. In 1794 he married a fellow American, Ruth Fairchild,[123] and together they had 10 children. In 1802 he was appointed a Justice of the Peace and Magistrate by the acting lieutenant-governor of Upper Canada. He was also the first post-master in the Delaware area.

He fought as a Captain in the War of 1812. After the war, he was forcibly captured by the Americans, taken to a prison in the US. He escaped and returned to work in the fur-trading business.

A newspaper report from about fifty years after Daniel's death summarizes his life as follows

> Daniel was a man of great vigour and enterprise who explored the forests and secured a location for a future home in Delaware Twp. He found many of the Indians encamped on its banks who traded with him. The Indians were well pleased with the white settler and named him Wabasash, signifying a good man or a wise man. He took up land on the flats and began to hew out a home for himself and at length other white people came and located there also. So utterly wild and unclaimed was the region at that time that the bears could be seen from the dwellings going to the river to drink, and the wolves in the swamps not far off "made night hideous" with their howling. The country was overrun with them. While the Government gave

---

[123] Ruth's ancestors had come to Turtle Island in the early 1600s.

> *a bounty for their destruction the settlers gave additional rewards and formed themselves into personal associations for the purpose of hunting and destroying them.*[124]

Unfortunately, there are no records that I could find to clarify which language his Indigenous name came from, let alone how he related with the nations he came to know.

The government of Ontario documents the area around Delaware as being part of Treaty 21 in 1819.[125] This treaty, known as the Longwoods Treaty, is known as one of the first which includes an annuity of $2,400 rather than a lump-sum payment to the local nation. In that year, Daniel, his wife, Ruth, and their 10 children were living on the land. It is unclear whether he would have been involved in the treaty process in any way; there is a small chance he may been involved informally or formally as a translator. Regardless, he would have heard about the treaty that was being signed for land they were already living on.

Years after Daniel died, the government brought in the hastily written "Williams Treaties" of the 1920s, which also cover the Delaware area. These treaties were an attempt to create a legal basis for the already well-established settlements in the area.[126]

---

[124] Excerpt from The London Free Press, Tuesday, February 27, 1877, reprinted in the London Leaf. Accessed via Ancestry.com.
[125] Government of Ontario, First Nations and Treaties Map. https://files.ontario.ca/treaties_map_english.pdf.
[126] See section 3 for further background.

16. 61+ Crossings: "It's complicated"

William Bain, Brita Mattsdotter, Peter Rambo, and Daniel Springer: these are a few of many immigrants from whom I am descended. While Peter and Brita were among the first for whom I have records of immigration from the Old World, many of my ancestors made the life-changing decision to cross the Atlantic Ocean and travel to the "New World."

As part of this process, I've realized that I—and those who ask me about this project—have an interest in "firsts." They, and I, want to know the first to arrive on Turtle Island, to Canada, or to British Columbia.

For all my ancestors, there was a "first" moment—a moment of arrival on these lands. Far enough back, there will be an "original" Bain, Rambo, Bennoit: a person who crossed the Atlantic Ocean to land somewhere on Turtle Island. So far in this narrative, I've documented several of those "firsts." "Firsts" to Turtle Island refer to the first to immigrate and also the first to settle, the first to colonize.

If I were to source out all these first-generation immigrants in my ancestry, how many would there be? From the research I've been able to do, here is a listing of my ancestors who moved from one side of the Atlantic to the other in their lifetime. I've grouped them by my four grandparents:

- Ian Bain's ancestors: 15 recorded crossings (not including two people[127] recorded as born on Turtle Island whose ancestors either came to Turtle Island at some point or were Indigenous)
- Claudia Barker's ancestors: 38 recorded crossings (not including two people[128] recorded as born on Turtle Island)
- Roy Jelly's ancestors: eight recorded crossings
- Marjorie Edwards's ancestors: two recorded crossings

I note a total of 63 crossings over a period of almost 300 years, not including any crossings associated with four people for whom there are no ancestry records.

Also remarkable is what I did not find, at least in our direct ancestral line, and not in the official records. I found family members who originated from only a few countries: England, Scotland, Ireland, Germany, Sweden, Netherlands, and France. I found no record of ancestors hailing from other parts of Europe (Eastern and Southern Europe), let alone ancestors from anywhere beyond the European subcontinent. I didn't find ancestors who were enslaved in the Americas. I also didn't find ancestors who were Indigenous.

It's possible my family lineage does not include anyone at all outside of northern Europe. In that case, the fact that my ancestors lived for 300+ years on Turtle Island, often significantly outnumbered by Indigenous peoples, suggests a remarkable segregation and separation between European settlers and non-European settlers or Indigenous peoples. To maintain cultural homogeneity by marrying

---

[127] If you're curious, those people are Dorcas Bragdon (b. 1695) and Anne Hooper (b. 1770).
[128] Still curious? Hannah Beach (b. 1659), and Mary Dempsey (b. 1711).

only within a Northern European background for 300+ years would be remarkable indeed.

The second possibility is that there were, in fact, intermarriages with peoples of non-northern European descent, but I haven't been able to find records in existing sources. Data in the sources I have searched, primarily online, tends to be predominantly from English-speaking and European origins, and I have not accessed oral histories that might reveal further information and context.

The third possibility is that intermarriages did happen, but the records of these marriages were never made, are missing, or the details of those peoples' ancestry were hidden either by authorities or by families. For most of the history of Turtle Island, ancestry from anywhere outside of northern Europe was, to varying degrees, obfuscated or disguised, rather than celebrated. If my ancestors intermarried with enslaved or Indigenous peoples, the absence of a record is, in itself, a relationship—a relationship of secrecy.

Recently I completed a DNA test in pursuit of further answers, and perhaps I should not be surprised that the results came back revealing ancestry in England, Scotland, Wales, Sweden, and Norway. Again, nothing outside of northern Europe. The possibility is strong that my ancestors kept to themselves, ethnically, at least when it came to marriage.

Firsts are like Christopher Columbus, one person through whom so many others entered, colonised, and irrevocably changed life and land on Turtle Island. Since Peter and Brita arrived in the early 1600s, there have been 11 generations of descendants born on Turtle Island soil. Using a conservative estimate of three surviving children born in each generation, it follows that there would be about 177,147 descendants by my parents' generation (the 1950s). Even counting only two children per generation, that would amount to 2,048 descendants by the 1950s.

Whether Peter and Brita are ancestors to thousands, or hundreds of thousands, what is clear is that their story is a part of a broader pattern across this land. My ancestors, along with many others, came as settlers; they cleared land, built homes, acquired title to Indigenous land, and had families. They brought and enforced their own legal systems and forms of governance.

Decimated by the combined weight of wars, slaughters, and diseases from the Eurasian continent, Indigenous populations plummeted in the years after Europeans arrived. Across Turtle Island, my ancestors flourished while Indigenous populations were decimated.

Part 3.
Arrivals on Coast Salish Territory, 1890–1920s

17. Coast Salish territory and Snauq

This narrative began on Jedediah Island on the coast of BC, moved back in history, and now returns once again to the western coast of Turtle Island. Around the turn of the 20th century, some of my ancestors found themselves on the traditional, ancestral and unceded territory of the Musqueam, Squamish, and Tsleil-wa-teuth. They lived in Mount Pleasant, a community within the city of Vancouver.

Since time immemorial, the area now known as Vancouver has been home to several Indigenous communities. Local chiefs spoke out too : in 1906 a Squamish chief known as Kiyapalanexw (Anglicized as Capilano) went with two other BC chiefs all the way to England to present a petition to Edward VII concerning Indigenous rights to the land. Here's an excerpt from the petition:

> To His Most Gracious Majesty King Edward VII,
>
> *Perhaps we are amongst the most remote of your majesty's subjects, yet we give place to none in our loyalty and devotion to your majesty's person, and to the British crown.*
>
> *[...] Sir James Douglas told us that large numbers of white people would come to our country, and in order to prevent trouble he designated large tracts of land for our use, and told us that if any white people encroached upon those lands he would remove them, which he did [...] But when Sir James Douglas was no longer governor other white people settled upon our lands and titles were issued to them by the British Columbian government. We have appealed to*

> the Dominion government which is made up of men elected by the white people who are living on our lands [...]
>
> We have our families to keep the same as the white man, and we know how to work as well as the white man; then why should we not have the same privileges as the white man?[129]

And yet despite this and other letters, Indigenous peoples continued to be affected by the decisions of "men elected by the white people who are living on our lands."

As far as I was able to ascertain, the communities closest to my ancestors' homes in Mount Pleasant were at Xwayxway and Snauq.

Xwayxway, or Whoi Whoi, as it was called in English, was located near what is now called Lumberman's Arch in the area known as Stanley Park. The community that lived there had been several hundred people strong but, after being ravaged by smallpox, was likely closer to 100 people. The village is said to be the site at which Captain George Vancouver was welcomed in 1792. Unfortunately, in 1888 the site upon which Xwayxway sat—a four-acre midden of discarded shells, tools, and other signs of human habitation—was dug up and ground down to give the park road a white sheen. At the same time, the last two houses in the village were burned. The last residents of Stanley Park were removed from the park by 1923, leaving no trace of their occupancy.[130]

---

[129] Taken from http://scoutmagazine.ca/2013/05/02/you-should-know-more-about-local-first-nations-leader-icon-joe-capilano/.
[130] "5 Secret Stories from Stanley Park"; https://forbiddenvancouver.ca/2017/06/06/five-secret-stories-from-stanley-park/.

While the communities of Stanley Park had been removed, by 1910 the Snauq reserve, at what is now known as Vanier Park near the mouth of False Creek, was a thriving, active community established on land defined by the Canadian government as reserve lands. The centerpiece of the community was a 150-foot longhouse made of cedar with an earthen floor. It must have been an impressive sight. A Methodist minister who spent Sundays at the Snauq reserve described "quite a settlement at Chief George's False Creek Reserve, probably a dozen houses, built of split cedar, saw boards and slabs, and the big community house; a total population, perhaps, of fifty persons all told. It was a settlement of consequence."[131]

Snauq was the region and area around the mouth of False Creek. In the days before colonization, False Creek itself was much larger. The mouth was over a kilometre across, and the waters reached all the way to modern Clark Drive, just below Mount Pleasant, and from 2nd Avenue to Dunsmuir Avenue. The flats and lands around the creek were home to sea asparagus, blue and white camas bulbs, and berry-picking spots. Snauq itself was known as the "supermarket" of the area. It was accessed by the Squamish, Musqueam, and Tsleil-wa-teuth seasonally. After the smallpox epidemic, the Tsleil-wa-teuth were left with less than 50 members. Somewhere between 1821 and the 1850s, Chief George Chipkaym of the Squamish nation set up a permanent settlement at Snauq; his son August Jack Khatsahlano was born there.[132]

---

[131] Rev. C.M. Tate in conversation with Matthews, 1 July 1932, in Matthews, Conversations, 158-9, 171. As cited in Barman, Jean (1996). *The West beyond the West: a history of British Columbia* (Rev. ed.). Toronto: University of Toronto Press.

[132] Lee Maracle, "Goodbye Snauq", in *Our Story: Aboriginal Voices of Canada's Past* (2004), pp. 205-219.

By the 1910s, the thriving villages of Snauq, which were visible from the English Bay bathing beach, became an item of public discussion. Jack Khatsahlano spoke about what happened next: "After the trees came down, houses went up, more mills, hotels, shantytowns until we were vastly outnumbered and pressured to leave. BC was so white then. So many places were forbidden to Indians, dogs, Blacks, Jews, and Chinamans."[133] The front cover of the August 1913 Western Call newspaper presents a strong, and commonly held, perspective on "Indian reserves" remaining near Vancouver at that point:

> *There are four Indian Reserves bordering on the Harbor of Vancouver—Kitsilano, Capilano, Seymour and Mission Reserves ... It is evident to all who give the subject thought that they cannot be left as at present; they are not suitable locations for the Indians, being too close to the city, therefore we ask, what shall be done with them? ... The citizens want action. The harbor must be developed. To do this we must have these Reserves.*

In fact, this perspective was shared by then Prime Minister Wilfrid Laurier, who stated in Parliament in April 1911 that, "where a reserve is in the vicinity of a growing town, as is the case in several places, it becomes a source of nuisance and an impediment to progress." The Indian Act was amended so that, "in the interest of the public and of the Indians of the band for whose use the reserve is held," reserves within or adjoining cities of at least 8,000 people could be removed.[134]

---

[133] Ibid, p. 213.
[134] Wilfrid Laurier in House of Commons debate, 19 April 1911, House of Commons Debates, 1910-11: 7249.

Any record of the voices of residents of the reserve speaks to the strength of their opposition to being forcibly moved. In 1904, the Indian Agent for Snauq records this:

> Chief says that he does not want to sell the land because it belonged to his Grandfather ... He didn't want to leave this place where he was born and it is the place where his dead relatives are buried—none of the men on the place want to sell it—the Queen gave him and his people the land.[135]

In 1913, building on the wave of popular opinion against the reserve, the government of BC entered into the fray. Despite the fact that Indigenous lands were a federal responsibility, the provincial government attempted to shortcut due process by purchasing the reserve. A local magistrate, fluent in the Chinook trade jargon spoken by the Squamish, gathered the heads of households and offered them a sum far below market value for the land. When they refused the cheques, they were told that if they didn't take this money, they would not get any, and that they would be "driven off by the police" if they did not accept.[136]

Later that same day, the attorney general bragged about the unfair price he had offered to the nation, calling it "one of the best real estate transactions ever carried out in the province," and stating that "this very valuable property ... should net us a million dollars profit."[137]

---

[135] R.C. McDonald, Indian Agent, quoted in "Reasons for Judgment," 42. As cited in Barman, Jean (1996). *The West beyond the West: a history of British Columbia* (Rev. ed.). Toronto: University of Toronto Press.

[136] Lee Maracle, "Goodbye Snauq" in *Our Story: Aboriginal Voices of Canada's Past* (2004), pp. 205–219.

[137] "An Act of Greatest Benefit to Vancouver," *Province*, 9 April 1913. As cited in Barman, Jean (1996). *The West beyond the West: a history of British Columbia* (Rev. ed.). Toronto: University of Toronto Press.

That's right—the very person responsible for negotiations with the community at Snauq had the audacity to acknowledge publicly the scale of his exploitation. Even by standards of fair sale at the time, the coercive Snauq purchase was exploitative.

Some voices spoke out against this egregious act. One Victoria newspaper called it "the greatest scandal in the history of the Provincial government of British Columbia," and liable to "a term in the penitentiary" if undertaken by "an individual in the community." However, at the time the land deal stood, and the Squamish residents of Snauq were forcibly removed by barge, their longhouses burned as they left[138]. They were not allocated additional reserve lands; most moved to the Squamish River valley or to North Vancouver.

In other words, just a few years after my ancestors Harry and Mary Ann Foote built a house at 12th and Alberta, the only remaining Indigenous community within Vancouver city limits was forcibly removed from the area. In contrast, the Foote house stands till today, and title to that land has never been questioned or revoked.

---

[138] Generations later, approximately half of the core Snauq lands came to be known as Vanier Park; the other half are privately held land. In 2000, the Squamish Nation and federal government at last settled claims related to reserves (not to Indigenous title to the land more broadly). The agreement gave the Squamish nation access to 10 acres in the shape of a 'Y' under the Burrard Bridge, known as the "railway lands." This parcel is a small portion of the 80 or so acres once occupied by the Snauq community.

18. A Flood of Settlers

My ancestors were a continuation of a growing flood of settlers to Vancouver during the time when the Snauq settlement was erased. Harry and Mary Ann Foote were the first of my ancestors to arrive from Portage La Prairie in 1890. Later came Jacob Bain and his children (Mabel, Nell, and Will); and, finally, by 1909, the Australian adventurer Morrison Jelly.

In 1886, Vancouver was incorporated as a city with only 1,000 residents. That same year, it was razed to the ground with the Great Fire of 1886. When Harry and Mary Ann entered the city in 1890, it was a quickly growing community whose population had already exploded to around 14,000 people.

At that point, downtown Vancouver was mostly dirt roads with occasional huge stumps, remnants of the rainforest that had, until a few decades earlier, covered the entire peninsula. From downtown, a track went south: Main Street. A trestle bridge crossed the False Creek flats, and then the road went up into Mt. Pleasant.

Several roads met at the top of the hill. The Fraser road headed down south, up over the hill into the forest, to the Fraser River. Kingsway trail, used by Indigenous peoples for many years, was now a thoroughfare to the much larger city of New Westminster. Where there once were Douglas fir, red cedar, and salal thickets, now there were fallen trees, stumps, the rough cut of new dirt roads. Across the city, wide, square lots were carved from forest.

1890 – View looking north on Main from 7th Ave before the fill. [139]

Broadway and Kingsway: a scene bustling with people, horses, and carts. Goods from the train up to the hill, from the homes down to the train. The scents of cut wood, mud, grease, a whiff of burning coal and a touch of malted beer all mixed together. The area was a construction zone, with houses rising from the stark black soil. There were few greens present, just brown and grey and the bright golden glow of freshly sawn lumber. There is a story that the English writer Rudyard Kipling purchased a parcel of land at the corner of 11th and Fraser on a brief visit to the city; he was a foreign speculator and made a good profit on a quick sale. Rapid change, great hopes, "new" land.

All this logging, all this settlement. And yet, whose lands were these? As is acknowledged now at the start of almost all public meetings in Coast Salish territories, the area now known as Vancouver has

---

[139]   VPL Number: 36. Photographer: H.T. Devine.

been occupied by the Musqueam, Squamish, and Tseil-wa-teuth nations since "time immemorial." No treaties were signed, and the land known as Vancouver remains "unceded," meaning there were never any written or verbal agreements that articulated the rights of settlers to Indigenous lands.

When George Vancouver arrived in Vancouver on June 13, 1792, he was welcomed by a chief who probably resided at Snauq, at what is now Kitsilano Point. His voyage, in 1792, came 10 years after the great smallpox epidemic of 1782. While exact numbers are hard to determine, it is likely that a significant proportion of the population of the area died in the epidemic. It is hard to imagine the scale and depth of such a devastating disease on entire communities with no natural immunity. His notes record the story of one such encounter:

> *We found one man, who had suffered very much from the small pox. This deplorable disease is not only common, but it is greatly to be apprehended as very fatal amongst them ... it may be somewhat premature to conclude that this delightful country has always been thus thinly inhabited; on the contrary, there are reasons to believe it has been infinitely more populous. Each of the deserted villages was nearly, if not quite, equal to contain all the scattered inhabitants we saw.*[140]

In Halq'eméylem, the language of the Stó:lō, Europeans are called "xwelítem," meaning "hungry people" or "starving people," which may be a reference to the ill-prepared gold prospectors who depended

---

[140] Stó:lō Heritage Trust. (2001). *A Stó:lō-Coast Salish Historical Atlas*. (K. T. Carlson, Ed.). Vancouver: Douglas & McIntyre, p. 86.

on Stó:lō generosity during the early years of settlement in BC.[141] The word xwelítem also has a broader metaphorical meaning, as in "to be hungry and greedy, driven by consumption and lacking respect, reverence and reciprocity for the land."[142]

---

[141] Carlson, Keith, *You Are Asked To Witness: The Stó:lô In Canada's Pacific Coast History* (1997).

[142] Heaslip, Robyn, *From Xwelítem Ways Towards Practices of Ethical Being in Stó:lō Téméxw: A Narrative Approach to Transforming Intergenerational White Settler Subjectivities* (2017), p. iii.

19. Bain Aunts in Kerrisdale: Mabel and Nell, 1910s–1920s

Jacob Bain (1845–1926) and Charlotte Simpson (1842–1905)				
Nell Bain (b. 1879)	**Mabel Bain (b. 1881)**	Elliot Bain (b. 1882) + Gertrude Coffin	Gordon Bain (b. 1883) + Alice Louise Hayward	**William Simpson Bain (b. 1886) + Kathleen E. Griffiths**

In early 1910, on Musqueam territory (Kerrisdale, Vancouver) lived a family from Epekwitk (PEI): older Jacob Bain, mourning the loss of his wife, and his three unmarried adult children: Nell, Mabel, and Will.

Like me, Nell was a teacher. She worked at Dawson School in downtown Vancouver. Being a schoolteacher was a common occupation for young unmarried women at the time. By the 1920s, Vancouver schools were becoming overcrowded; most high school classes had between 35 and 40 students, particularly in the less-affluent East Side. Some things don't change, it seems!

Nell would not have had Indigenous students in her classes, however. By 1920, the Canadian federal government passed legislation making it mandatory for all "Indian" children in BC seven years or older to attend residential schools or their parents would face fines and prison terms.[143] The nearest residential schools to Vancouver were St. Mary's in Mission or St. George's in Lytton, BC. In these schools, children were separated from their parents, grandparents, and community. They were forbidden to speak their own language and often worked long hours of forced labour.

By the 1930s there was significant evidence that residential schools were causing significant harm. A 1907 report by government medical inspector P.H. Bryce reported that 24 percent of previously healthy Indigenous children were dying in residential schools—not including children who were sent home critically ill and then died at home.[144] In 1913, Duncan Campbell Scott, then Deputy Superintendent-General of Indian Affairs, wrote: "It is quite within the mark to say that fifty per cent of the children who passed through these schools did not live to benefit from the education which they had received therein."[145] Despite these words, local residential schools remained open until the 1980s[146].

The school Nell worked in would have been a different story: while schooling was strict and basic, children went home every evening to their families, were not forced into manual labour, and did not, as far as I'm aware, face increased mortality rates as a result of their

---

[143] Historical Issues: Canada's Bureaucratic Colonization of Indigenous Peoples." No One Is Illegal Vancouver. 2007. <http://noii-van.resist.ca> March 2008.
[144] Indigenous Foundations: The Residential School System; https://indigenousfoundations.arts.ubc.ca/the_residential_school_system/.
[145] As quoted by Schwartz, Daniel (2015) "Truth and Reconciliation Commission: By the Numbers". https://www.cbc.ca/news/indigenous/truth-and-reconciliation-commission-by-the-numbers-1.3096185.
[146] The residential school at Lytton, which for most of its life was known as St. George's, opened in 1902 and closed finally in 1979. St. Mary's Indian Residential School, located in Mission, BC, was opened in 1863 and was the last residential school in BC to close, in 1985, a total of 122 years.

education. Nell's students would have been settlers, not Indigenous-identified students. It's hard to know whether she would have had contact with or even awareness of the residential schools then operating in Mission and Lytton.

In family stories, I hear of Mabel and Nell as independent, creative, independent, quirky, unmarried aunts. As my grandmother put it, with mixed admiration and envy, "these ladies never married and kept so busy at their professions that they hired a person for housekeeping."[147]

Mabel seems to have been a bit more of an adventurer than her sister Nell. She was the second daughter and the first to move out of the family home in PEI. When she was 20 years old, she had left home to lodge in the "big city," Charlottetown. She painted oils of landscapes and scenery. She studied art in Los Angeles and San Diego, California,[148] before moving to BC with her father and siblings.

Mabel's "day job" was the art form of her time: she was a milliner, or hat-maker, at Unique Hat Shoppe. Her tall, shiny black cabinet—two tall sets of drawers, square and polished, flanking a long, oval mirror—sat at the entrance of my grandmother's house for as long as I can remember. Her clients would have sat in front of the mirror on a small stool, hat on head, while she cut and twisted and arranged the cloth, lace, and bows to suit the client's taste and latest fashion.

However, Mabel is best known as a talented painter, so I've always imagined Mabel in her work as an artist in beautiful West Coast rainforests. She rode her horse to places she liked to paint, to the

---

[147] Bain, C.A. *Lilies of my field*. Vancouver, 2006, p. 144.
[148] Dictionary of Canadian Artists by McDonald, cited in *Lilies of My Field*, p. 161.

parks of North Vancouver and Golden Ears. She must have ridden from Kerrisdale through the gullies and ravines of the West Side, all the way to New Westminster, and from there, on muddy trails past clanging sawmills. Crossing the river, horse balking and paints clanking, she rode for miles. Her solid, dark leather painting case was etched with deep scratches from being carried on horseback for hours. Her paintings speak to a deep appreciation of the land, trees, and mountainscapes.

Painting by Mabel Bain at Lighthouse Park, North Vancouver.

I found records documenting a short trip Mabel took "abroad" on a boat from Victoria to Seattle, Washington. I imagine her in bright colours, off-kilter hat accenting a saucy, light-haired bob. She was five feet 11 inches, a tall woman by any measure, and a good four inches taller than the average male of her generation.[149] Though 42 years old at the time, she wrote a confident "38 years" on the customs and immigration form—perhaps because her companions, Mary and Hazel, were in their mid-twenties.[150]

Around the same time that Mabel and Nell were living their independent lives, another female West Coast artist was making a name for herself in Victoria, BC: Emily Carr, who remains perhaps the most famous female artist in BC history. Emily Carr's work explicitly referenced and engaged with Indigenous arts and history, documenting the totem poles of Haida Gwaii and Kwakwawak'w lands, for example. There is no record of a connection between Mabel and Emily Carr, but it is likely that Mabel would have heard about the work of another, much better known, West Coast female artist.

---

[149] Just because I had to look: the average male born in the 1880s in Canada was five feet seven inches; 100 years later, in the 1980s, the average was five feet 10 inches. She would be considered tall even in the modern age.

[150] Her companions were Mary Barr (25 years old, five feet five inches, with brown hair) and Hazel McRome (23 years old, five feet four inches).

20. Will Bain: From War to Treaty 5, 1915–1920s

In addition to Mabel and Nell, there was another young Bain on Coast Salish territory, Will Bain. In his early twenties he lived with his older sisters until he started earning his own money. He became an electrician and a gas engineer. Just after Christmas of 1915, he voluntarily enlisted in the war effort:

> **OATH TO BE TAKEN BY MAN ON ATTESTATION.**
>
> I, ...William Simpson Bain................................., do make Oath, that I will be faithful and bear true Allegiance to His Majesty **King George the Fifth**, His Heirs and Successors, and that I will as in duty bound honestly and faithfully defend His Majesty, His Heirs and Successors, in Person, Crown and Dignity, against all enemies, and will observe and obey all orders of His Majesty, His Heirs and Successors, and of all the Generals and Officers set over me. So help me God.
>
> ....*W. S. Bain*............(Signature of Recruit)
>
> Date......Jan. 4th............191 6.   ....*E. Clough*............(Signature of Witness)

Will Bain War Oath.[151]

Will survived the war and, upon coming back to Canada, was awarded a piece of land to call his own—a "veteran's benefit," they called it. On June 9, 1919, he went to Edmonton, Alberta, to access a loan of $7,000, which included $4,000 for the "purchase" of a quarter-section of land, about 160 acres. This parcel of prairie land was foreign to Will, as he had been raised in PEI and spent his twenties in Vancouver.

---

[151] Canada, Soldiers of the First World War, 1914-1918. From ancestry.ca.

Loan document given by Soldier Settlement Board to William Bain.

While on duty in England, Will had met a young woman by the name of Kathleen Griffiths. She was, according to my grandmother, the "belle of the ball" in her day. She recorded her profession as "news agent" when they married in the spring of 1918 in her hometown of Dymock, Gloucestershire, several hours west of London.

William and Kathleen wedding record, Gloucestershire.[152]

Will left first, to prepare the farm for her; Kathleen followed by ship and train to meet Will in Alberta, where she would live in a place more isolated than any she had ever imagined. The plot of land was located near Ranfurly, which today is on the Yellowhead Highway about one hour and 20 minutes' drive east of Edmonton. In those days, the 130-kilometre trip to the "city" would have been a two-day horse and buggy ride away. Kathleen's first full prairie winter, with chin-deep snow and a young baby to feed, must have been an experience unlike any other. The land Will had received was what some call "hardscrabble" land: barren or barely arable land. Eking sustenance out of that land required long, grueling hours of back-breaking labour for Will and Kathleen.

Will Bain in front of his Ranfurly home.

---

[152] From Gloucestershire Archives; Gloucester, England; Reference Numbers: P125 IN 1/28.

Kathleen stayed on the isolated Alberta farm for seven years before returning to England. She moved back and forth between England and Alberta several times but never did move back in with Will, though she stayed in touch over the years, from Edmonton and Vancouver. She rented rooms in Edmonton and her son Ian lived with her briefly during his university years. She was a bit of a mysterious figure, not often spoken of in family stories. In later years, she would write to Ian from time to time, asking for money. Ian's wife, my grandmother, reported with disapproval that she may have been a member of the Bahá'í faith.

Will stayed in Ranfurly after Kathleen left, farming and raising Ian as a single father. Paintings of the farm hung on the wall of my grandmother's kitchen for as long as I can remember. The paintings were made by Mabel Bain, she said, and depict scenes with long grasses and tall trees, in pale yellows, greens, and browns. In one of the paintings is a tow-haired boy, Ian Bain, son of Will.

The "veteran's benefit" land Will had been awarded was part of Treaty 6 territory. This treaty was signed in 1876, by representatives of the Crown and Lieutenant Governor of Manitoba and the North-West Territories, with what they called the Plain and Wood Cree Tribes of Indians, which included over 40 nations. Curious to understand more, I found a copy of Treaty 6, replete with long, finely penned lines of English legalese:

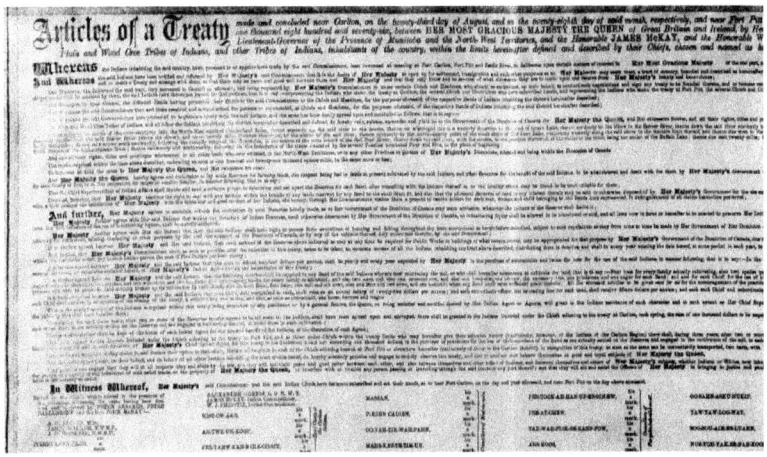

A portion of the original parchment of Treaty 6.[153]

In one of the middle lines of small print, the treaty includes the following statement:

> The Plain and Wood Cree Tribes of Indians, and all the other Indians inhabiting the district hereinafter described and defined, do hereby cede, release, surrender and yield up to the Government of the Dominion of Canada, for Her Majesty the Queen and Her successors forever, all their rights, titles and privileges, whatsoever, to the lands included within the following limits, that is to say ... [154]

---

[153] From Treaties, Surrenders and Agreements archive IT 297. Accessed at http://www.collectionscanada.gc.ca/databases/treaties/001040-119.01-e.php?&sisn_id_nbr=297&interval=20&&PHPSESSID=2htqc9j6k8opg2cfgj2mjbkpi107n0qii7dt4kch-p67aj7jauojo.

[154] From http://www.aadnc-aandc.gc.ca/eng/1100100028710/1100100028783.

The written text of Treaty 6, like each of the "numbered" treaties, is a description of the colonial government's interpretation of the negotiations. It's important to remember, though, that agreement to the treaty itself is not equivalent to the words on the written document. As stated by Sharon Venne:

> The Elders have long disputed many aspects of the government of Canada's version of Treaty 6. The main criticism of the written version has to do with the language used about the lands. The written version contains the wording "cede, surrender, and forever give up title to the lands." The Elders maintain that these words were not included in the original treaty. The Chiefs and Elders could not have sold their lands to the settlers as they could only share the lands, according to the Cree, Saulteaux, Assiniboine and Dene laws. When the Elders were told of these written words, they had difficulty understanding them. These words do not exist in their languages.[155]

A familiar story by now: the colonial government, as a veteran's benefit, gave Will lands for "free" that were part of a region governed by contested treaties.

While Will was provided with land and recognition on his return, "Indian" soldiers serving in the same war received a less-than-warm embrace. In the First World War, approximately one-third of the total male population of First Nations aged 18–45 enlisted in the war, the highest enlistment rate of any cultural group in Canada.[156] This is an incredibly high number: and this occurred in spite of the fact that the

---

[155] Sharon H. Venne, "Understanding Treaty 6: An Indigenous Perspective" in M. Asch, ed., *Aboriginal and Treaty Rights in Canada* (2002). As quoted by http://digital.scaa.sk.ca/ourlegacy/exhibit_treaties.

[156] From Aboriginal Contributions During the First World War, https://www.aadnc-aandc.gc.ca/eng/1414152378639/1414152548341.

Indian Act did not give Indigenous peoples the full rights of citizenship, such as the vote. During the war itself, Indigenous solders were treated on par with other soldiers, fighting literally shoulder to shoulder.

When soldiers returned, they learned that the Indian Act (at the time) removed Indian status from any individual who stayed off-reserve for longer than four years. Participation in the war often meant that soldiers returned to their reserve communities without rights to membership in the band or access to lands.

To add insult to injury, across the prairies, a total of 85,000 acres were directly taken from Indian reserves for non-Indigenous soldier settlement as part of the Soldier Settlement Act. Voices at the time spoke out against this as yet one more way the federal government was taking away Indigenous lands. Frank Cahill, Member of Parliament for Pontiac, Quebec, said:

> *There are thousands and millions of acres of vacant land throughout the West owned by large corporations, and why we should take from the Indian his rights, while he is living on the land in his own way, to make way for settlers or renters, and leave to the large corporations their lands which they are holding for profit, is a mystery to me. I think if we are going to do any confiscating of land for the benefit of the white man, you should take the white man's land.*[157]

The Soldier Settlement Board proceeded to work alongside the Department of Indian Affairs to successfully allocate reserve lands to white veterans, writing yet another sad episode in the long history of dispossession of Indigenous peoples.[158]

---

[157] NA, RG 10, vol. 11205, file 1, transcripts of debates in Hansard, 1918, 7, (F.S. Cahill).
[158] http://www.mhs.mb.ca/docs/mb_history/37/infamousproposal.shtml#021.

Will Bain continued to stay in contact with his Vancouver family, particularly his father, through his Alberta years. Eventually, Will left the Ranfurly farm to live closer to family on Coast Salish territory.

21. Letters from Vancouver in the 1920s

> *"... I have lived longer than most people yet it seems but a very short time since I was a child ..."*
>
> — Letter from Jacob Bain (Vancouver) to his son Will Bain (Ranfurly, Alberta)

I read the sentence above sitting in my grandmother's apartment in Burnaby, BC. It was a Saturday morning in June—a bit rainy, somewhat mild—and I had brought along my copy of her book. I had helped with the memoir, but the writing was all hers. And now, reading again, I noticed several short quotes from letters by Jacob Bain. "Where are the rest?" I asked. "How many letters are there? Do you have them? Can I read them?"

> "They're a bit tedious, to be honest," she said. "He must have been getting on in years; he goes on and on about the weather."
>
> "Let me see, Grandma. I'd be interested to see them, to glance through what's there."

She took them out of a bigger envelope—a slightly torn, re-used envelope, something saved from a mail-out years ago. Inside were multiple little old envelopes, stamps still intact, faded blue lettering shakily naming the addressee—Will Bain—and the return name, a tiny hand-scripted Jacob Bain.

The letters were folded several times vertically and then again horizontally, so the multiple pages would fit into their too-small envelopes. Jacob wrote his letters in precisely angled blue ink. Sentences follow sentences in orderly, reliable rows across the front and then the back of the page.

Jacob, son of the "first Bain" to Turtle Island, William Bain, had grown up in Epekwitk (PEI). He and his wife, Charlotte, had married in their thirties, quite late for the time, and had five children together. Charlotte died on Valentine's Day of 1905, 63 years old, just 30 kilometres from the place she was born.

Jacob, living in Kerrisdale with his daughters Mabel and Nell, wrote to his son Will, now a single father, in what he perhaps saw as an encouraging tone.

In this letter just before Christmas of 1922, he penned, "You have written that [you] are installing a Radio instrument in your house. I hope you will be successful in getting it to work satisfactory, you will not seem as entirely shut off from the outside world."

In another, he opines on the value of education for his grandchildren: "We will send Gordon's boy[159] to the high school for this year, after that if I have any say in the matter he must do something that he will learn how to make a living at. I don't think that he would ever do anything with an education anyways." I hope Gordon's young boy wasn't given such advice to his face.

The letters are folded in many pieces, each in their own stamped envelope, and each in scratchy longhand. Most have long and rather dry sections describing the weather, as my grandmother had noted. Why bother reading them all, I thought—and yet I was compelled,

---

[159] This would have been one of the sons of Jacob's brother Gordon, who had also moved to Vancouver several years earlier.

fascinated, soaking up the hand-scrawled words of a long-dead ancestor.

And then, partway through the stack of letters, this quote:

> "The lumber mills are dispensing with their Oriental labour and taking on white men, they say that white men are more satisfactory although their wages higher and it is a good thing for the labouring man."
>
> — Letter from Jacob Bain (Vancouver) to his son Will Bain (Ranfurly, Alberta) 1920s (exact date unknown)

I read it a few times, slowly, then quickly. I got out my laptop, typed out his letter, added the date and the place. The logic unfurled in front of me. "Oriental" labour is being "dispensed" with; white labour is somehow more "satisfactory." I note a few things. There's the problematic and undefinable "other" labelled the "Oriental"—and then there's the suggestion that lumber mills, and other places of employment, did in fact keep record of the "ethnic origin" of their employees. And to top it all off, lumber mills had decided to fire all those of one ethnic group, in favour of "white men": "they say that white men are more satisfactory although their wages higher."

This was only one small side-note in a letter, an off-hand comment about the news perhaps. But it was a window, for me, into what else what happening at that time in Vancouver. My great-great-grandfather suggests that "they"', implying commonly held views of the time, are saying that "white men" are somehow worth paying more money.

I was curious to learn more about the context of his comment. To explore what was actually happening in that time, I researched the employment records of a few local mills, looking for a mass dismissal.

Hastings Saw Mill had been set up in 1865. For the first 20 years, the majority of workers were Indigenous and Chinese, but in 1886, white workers who had been employed in railway construction came to the mill. By 1902, there were 128 white employees and only 49 Chinese and Japanese employees. These records suggest a slow and significant switch in the workforce from Chinese/Indigenous to "white men" by the time Jacob wrote.

And yet the inequity was deep. Skin colour determined wage level directly. The manager of Royal City Mills in Vancouver gave the following evidence to a Royal Commission in 1902:

> *We employ 150 men, of whom 60 are Japanese. Over half the Japanese are paid 90 cents a day. Three Japanese have charge of saws. They are satisfactory. We get as much done as if run by a white man. We pay a Japanese sawyer $1.25 a day. We pay white labour of the same class (sawyers) $2.25 ... White men could not live on the same wages we pay Chinese and Japanese.*[160]

The recognition that white men could not live on the wages paid to Asian workers is striking; even more significant is the scale of the difference in wages between white and non-white workers. These structural inequalities were not only racist in themselves; they fueled further resentment of Asian workers, who were quite literally "cheap labour." The resentment was so strong that the then-premier of BC, coal miner James Dunsmuir, ran for election on the promise that he would replace all the Chinese employees at his Nanaimo coal site with white employees.

---

[160] Kobayashi & Jackson, "Japanese Canadians and the Racialization of Labour in the British Columbia Sawmill Industry." BC Studies (downloaded file).

By the early 1900s, British Columbian settler society had become increasingly and overtly racist toward Indigenous peoples, as well as toward Asian settlers. A head-tax on immigrants from China was in place, set at $50 in 1885. That was followed by the 1895 Provincial Elections Act of BC, which stated: "No Chinaman, Japanese or Indian shall have his name placed on the Register of Voters for any Electoral District, or be entitled to vote at any election."[161]

Public racism only increased after that point: in 1903, the head-tax on immigrants from China was increased from $50 to $500, the equivalent of two years' wages. In the Victoria Times a story described how "white boys have made an organized attempt to prevent Chinese pupils from attending the Rock Bay and Central Schools."[162] Soon after that, the Vancouver and Victoria school boards set up segregated schools for students of Asian ancestry.

And then, there was the race riot of 1907:

> The Asiatic Exclusion League was formed and, on a Saturday night, September 9 [1907], a great rally for the league took place ... A monster parade marched down Hastings Street that night ... someone shouted "on to Chinatown" and the trouble started ... On the first trip only rocks were thrown and hundreds of windows were broken. The second trip proved more vicious, for this time there was gunfire.[163]

---

[161] "From Racism to Redress: The Japanese Canadian Experience." The Canadian Race Relations Foundation. <http://www.crr.ca/> March 2008.

[162] "The Vancouver Riot" in *White Canada Forever: Popular Attitudes and Public Policy Toward Orientals in British Columbia*, McGill Queens University Press 2002, p. 63.

[163] From Albert Foote, "Vancouver Revolt Cost City $16,000", The *Vancouver Sun Magazine*, 6 September 1947; as quoted in *Vancouver: A City Album*, p. 59.

The focus of the riot was the Powell Street area, home to the majority of Vancouver's Japanese population. There is no way of knowing who was a part of the "monster parade" that evening, and whether any of those involved were my ancestors or their friends. However, it is very likely that they knew, were connected to, or at least had heard about the Asiatic Exclusion League.

A few years later, the Komagata Maru Incident occurred, involving a ship that arrived in Vancouver's harbor in 1914 with 376 passengers from India. Racism against Indian immigrants had led to the passage a few years earlier of a "continuous journey" law: while it technically stated that any passenger planning to land in Vancouver must not stop at any port of call along the route, the law had been specifically intended to prevent Indian immigration, since any trip from India would require at least one stop en route.

The Komagata Maru was moored in the Vancouver harbor for days, weeks, then months. The ship made front-page headlines day after day. After significant legal challenges, and two months of its passengers being detained on board, the ship was turned back to India. Upon its arrival in Calcutta, British authorities suspected the passengers of being there to cause trouble, and 20 passengers were killed, with 200 others imprisoned. The incident was a shocking and very public manifestation of the racism of the time.[164]

There was clearly a strong sense of British Columbia as "British" and therefore white. As one prominent journalist of the time put it:

---

[164] Johnston, Hugh. Komagata Maru. http://www.thecanadianencyclopedia.ca/en/article/komagata-maru/. Much has been written about the Komogata Maru incident—for example Renisa Mawani's *Across Oceans of Law*.

> *This vast and in some respects still unknown country has possibilities in store for it ... possibilities as a greater Britain on the Pacific, where British arts and institutions will expand under fresh impetus, where the British flag will forever fly, where British laws and justice will be respected and enforced, and where British men and women will be bred equal to the best traditions of the race.*[165]

By creating a hierarchy of races with Indigenous peoples as inferior, white settler colonists were ensuring their own position at the top of the hierarchy. As Robert Borden, then prime minister of Canada, put it: "British Columbia must remain a British and Canadian province, inhabited and dominated by men in whose veins runs the blood of those great pioneering races which built up and developed not only Western, but Eastern Canada."[166]

Back in Jacob's letter, I re-read one final line: "and it is a good thing for the labouring man." Decades later, his words are hard to read.

Jacob was by no means unusual for his time; he was commenting on happenings of the day, not causing or actively supporting the dismissal of workers. However, he did condone or even support hypothetical dismissal of workers of Asian background. He didn't, as far as we know, speak up against low wages and racist firings. Would I have? He was a product of his time, and, at the time, colonial rule involved exploitation of the labour that was available, as well as the erasure of Indigeneity.

---

[165] "The Komagata Maru Incident" in *White Canada Forever: Popular Attitudes and Public Policy Toward Orientals in British Columbia*, McGill Queens University Press 2002, pg. 93.

[166] "The Vancouver Riot" in *White Canada Forever: Popular Attitudes and Public Policy Toward Orientals in British Columbia*, McGill Queens University Press 2002, pg. 75.

Jacob lived in a different BC. And yet, the "British" Columbia he experienced was formative in creating the present-day life I live on Coast Salish territory. My task is to understand and challenge the ways in which those patterns continue to manifest in my own time.

Jacob and Will continued corresponding until Jacob's health became precarious. In 1926, Jacob died at the age of 81. Around that time Jacob's unmarried sisters, Mabel and Nell, made the decision to move to one of the oldest colonial settlements in British Columbia, Fort Langley.

22. Stó:lō territory: Fort Langley, 1920s

From Vancouver, farther up the river, white explorers had first traveled through the Fraser Valley by the early 1800s; however, the population had expanded significantly by the mid-1800s. As one Stó:lō witness put it, "Xwelitem, that's what the Indians call the white man, because in them days those white people travelling on the way to the gold rush, they were starving. Xwelitem, that means "starving." Well, the Indians began to feed them, feed them till they get all right."[167]

During the early days of the gold rush, when James Douglas was governor, the government had established a set of treaties with Indigenous people of southern Vancouver Island; many Stó:lō members had been present as witnesses at the signings. They saw these as agreements that "essentially created two types of reserves— one for Aboriginal people and one for Xwelitem immigrants (the latter type composed of the towns and settlements identified in the treaties themselves)".[168]

However, access to land beyond reserve lands was severely constrained in the years after Douglas. By 1867, the Chief Commissioner of Lands and Works, James Trutch, unilaterally reduced the size of reserve lands by 92 percent, without consultation. The standard became a maximum of 10 acres per family—this at a

---

[167] Stó:lō Heritage Trust. (2001). *A Stó:lō-Coast Salish Historical Atlas.* (K. T. Carlson, Ed.). Vancouver: Douglas & McIntyre. p. 85.
[168] Ibid.

time when individual settlers could pre-empt 160 acres and then purchase up to 480 more.[169]

Around the same time, the number of Indigenous families was reduced significantly as a result of the toll of European infectious diseases. The smallpox epidemic of 1862–1863 killed approximately 20,000 people out of the then-total of 60,000 Indigenous people in the province. The Indigenous population continued to decline rapidly over the decades to come, at exactly the time that settlers were flooding the land. When British Columbia entered Confederation in 1871, the population of BC was approximately 30 percent settler and 70 percent Indigenous; by 1914 the population was 95 percent non-Indigenous.[170]

Just about ten years before the Bains moved to Fort Langley, in 1910–1912, the Government of British Columbia established the McKenna-McBride Commission, which was tasked with resolving the "Indian reserve question" in British Columbia. As the commission was set up, a group of chiefs of the "Interior Tribes of BC" wrote a letter expressing the following:

> *From the very beginning our chief grievance has been what we state here in plain language to be the stealing of our lands by the BC Government. Our hearts have grown sour with the years on this question. It is a sore thing for us to see our country sold over our heads every day in the year ... above all we maintain the question of our title should be settled first. In this we simply ask justice, and our rights. We desire not what belongs to the whites nor anyone*

---

[169] Barman, Jean (1996). *The West beyond the West: a history of British Columbia* (Rev. ed.). Toronto: University of Toronto Press, p. 155.
[170] Ibid, p. 156.

else. We simply want what belongs to us. We claim we have a tribal ownership in all unsurrendered lands of this country. We also claim tribal ownership of all the game, and fisheries, and water, and in fact all natural resources in these tribal territories of ours. We are suffering a considerable loss in these lands being taken from us, and we want compensation for this loss.

Besides no man cares to have his belongings, specially that part from which he draws his life, taken from him without treaty or payment of any kind. Were we to act the same way with the possessions of the whites, would they stand for it? Would they submit? They would claim their rights in what had always belonged to themselves, and their forefathers, and would fight for it if need be. Although we have not the power, we are none the less proud, and we feel this injury keenly.[171]

While the commission had a very limited mandate to focus on reserves, as a part of those hearings, the chiefs spoke eloquently to their rights and title. The chief of the Langley band, for example, shared these words:

THE CHIEF: To-day I am telling you that I own the land, and it don't belong to anyone else—I own the land and I own the water. I have never had anyone to help me out with the Government or from anyone—the white men have taken our land and we have never got anything. During the time Simon Fraser came here my grandfather was up at Sapperton—when he came they were kind to him. Was

---

[171] 1913 (May) Statement of Chiefs of the Interior Tribes of British Columbia; as quoted in Stó:lō Heritage Trust. (2001). *A Stó:lō-Coast Salish Historical Atlas*. (K. T. Carlson, Ed.). Vancouver: Douglas & McIntyre, p. 179.

it because the Indians were too kind to him that the Government is not going to give us a square deal?

MR. COMMISSIONER MACDOWALL: *This question has been dealt with by the Government at Ottawa and they have decided to refer the question of Indian Title to the High Court of Canada with the right of an appeal to the Privy Council of England.*

THE CHIEF: *During Governor Seymour's time ... we were told that the Governor was going to give us some more land and give us reserves, and he said that the Government was going to pay the Indians for the outside lands and that was in his speech ... since that speech was made, we have never heard anything more about it, and I am tired waiting now for the compensation from the Government.*[172]

The Chief's frustration around Indigenous title was not dealt with by the governments of the time and remained unresolved as Mabel and Nell settled on that land. In fact, to this day, the Langley (now known as the Kwantlen), Stó:lō, and Matsqui have not signed treaties with the Province of BC. The land remains "unceded"; it has never legally changed hands.

In venues such as the McKenna-McBride Commission, the "official" focus was on minute changes in the size of tiny reserves allocated by the settler government. Even had the Indigenous-written letters been shared in public media at the time, it is unlikely they would have been framed positively. This was a time when the colonial attitude toward land was built on the assumption that giving land for free to newcomers to "settle" would "improve" the land.

---

[172] "Meeting with the Indians of Langley Band," p. 121. Accessed at McKenna-McBride Royal Commission, https://www.ubcic.bc.ca/mckenna_mcbride_royal_commission.

In sum, in terms of formal language, contemporary news, and prevailing attitudes, it is unlikely settlers in BC were exposed to significant content emphasizing the sovereignty of Indigenous peoples. This would have been true of Harry and Mary Ann Foote when they arrived in Vancouver in the 1890s, as well as for Will, Mabel and Nell Bain in Fort Langley of the 1930s.

By the 1930s, Fort Langley was long past its mid-1800s heyday, when the small wooden fort was temporarily made the capital of the new colony of British Columbia in 1858. By 1886 the Hudson's Bay Company had sold the fort, and in 1923 the site was officially commemorated by the Historic Sites and Monuments Board of Canada.[173] Then and now, the colonial fort retains its buildings and wooden wall defenses for the sake of school visitors and tourists. Just a few blocks up Mary Street from a present-day ice cream shop, Mabel and Nell had a house and extensive garden.[174]

While the Bain family moved upriver to Fort Langley by the 1930s, another family, the Jedediah-connected Foote family, remained in what is now known as Vancouver.

---

[173] Fort Langley National Historic Site of Canada Management Plan 2013, p. x.
[174] In the 1950s, Will Bain sold the farm in Alberta and built a small home for himself on Coast Salish territory, on the corner of Mabel and Nell's property in Fort Langley.

23. Mt. Pleasant, 1910s

Harry Foote (1859-1937) + Mary Ann Brooke (1864-1953)					
Henry Foote + Alice Foote	Olive Foote + Oscar Olmstead	Winnie Foote + Morris Jelly	Charles Foote + Bessie Hayes	F. Myrtle Foote + James King	Lister Foote

For the first years of their time on Coast Salish Territory, and during the early Jedediah years, Harry and Mary Ann Foote and family lived at 339 E. 9th Ave (now E. Broadway).[175] Their house stood across the street from an elementary school (now Kingsgate Mall), and just steps from the Broadway and Kingsway electric streetcars. In 1910, they hosted both Winnie's and Myrtle's weddings in their home.

In the 20 years since Harry and Mary Ann had moved to Coast Salish territory, settlement had expanded significantly. At the turn of the century, "100,000 men by 1910" was a slogan used by boosters of Vancouver. The growing population they were referencing was, of course, white Canadians.

After raising their family on Broadway, and after building a home on Jedediah Island, Harry and Mary Ann bought an empty lot in a new development at 12th and Alberta. At the time, Mt. Pleasant was a popular residential area.[176] As Mayor Neelands recollected, "At that

---

[175] From 1890 to 1898, they lived at 348 E. 9th, before moving to 339 E. 9th, now the site of a two-storey retail/residential property housing a Vietnamese restaurant (with delicious food).

[176] At this point city hall was located near Hastings and Main.

time ... Mt. Pleasant and Fairview were leading residential districts. There were no such places as Kitsilano, Shaughnessy, Kerrisdale, Grandview or Hastings ..."[177]

Harry and Mary Ann hired F. Strain to design the home and had it built by T. Williams for a total of $4,500, a value of almost $120,000 in 2018 dollars. In a photograph taken in 1910, they stand on the veranda of their new home, overlooking fresh paint, a raw dirt yard, and unfinished sidewalks.

2812 Alberta upon completion in 1910.[178]

---

[177] Mayor Thos F. Neelands, quoted in J.S. Matthews "Early Vancouver" vol. 5, p. 149, as quoted in *Vancouver: A City Album*, p. 64.
[178] Image from private collection of Eileen Bentley.

2812 Alberta. Photo: Eileen Bentley, 2014.

In a photo taken on the veranda, Harry Foote looks directly at the camera with a regal air seated in a high-backed chair made of shiny black mahogany with leather arms and back. His black leather lace-up boots are solid, substantial. His wife, Mary Ann, sits in a rocking chair, hands clasped. Her dress is made of thick fabric, replete with a long row of knotted black buttons on the left, a dark belt just below the bodice, and lace protruding from the long sleeves and high neck. Her dark hair is pulled up and back. Around her neck is a long cord with a house key. Her eyes look directly at the camera, with lips set confidently, as if she knows the photographer.

Foote family at 2812 Alberta. Standing: Cedric, Lister, Myrtle and Edgar; sitting: Winnie, Harry, Olive and Mary Foote. [179]

The Foote home still stands today on the now-busy 12th Avenue, at the southeast corner of the intersection with Alberta St. Trees and bushes have grown high around the edges, concealing the stone fencing. The gate at the southeast corner, now leaning and rusted, is the original piece as installed by the Footes. The current house itself maintains the same frame, but with the wide, sweeping lower veranda and the 2nd floor veranda now walled in for additional space.

From the Alberta Street side, sidewalks are worn, showing their skeleton of pebbles and stones. The entrance is guarded by tall, knobby-kneed rhododendrons—old enough to date back to the time of the Footes, perhaps. There is a soft green glow around the

---

[179] Photo from private collection of Eileen Bentley.

house—green moss, a mist of green algae on light-blue walls. The expansive wrap-around verandas are long gone: in their place a series of quick-panelled walls, and square, solid windows, turned into studio apartments.

A few years ago, I visited the house around Halloween. I left the sidewalk and approached the stairs. I got chatting with the owner, a down-to-earth drywaller, grey hair in a ponytail. His parents bought the house from the Footes in 1953, he thinks. He grew up in the house, lived there his whole life. The year I met him, his parents had died and so he was the new owner of the place, worth $2 million and change, he thought (much more now!). He invited me to come in and take a look around.

Door Handle, 2812 Alberta. Photo: Eileen Bentley.

Inside, I noted an aroma of old leather, long-held dust, and wooden walls. The doors were made of solid wood, with ornate metal handles polished by long usage. The stairs were now worn in the middle, sagging slightly beneath a hundred years of wear. The grand staircase had a well-polished banister, the kind kids would love to slide down.

The top two floors had four rooms, with one bathroom for the boarders to share. Next floor: four bedrooms, each with their own bathroom, now studio suites. The main floor was originally a grand dining hall and rooms for the Foote family; now it was divided, with porch and room space, into two smaller studios. The current owner rents out the suites/rooms and lives himself in a serpentine four-bedroom unit that encompasses the original main-floor kitchen, a sprawling basement/pool room, and a top-floor "meditation room" with a veranda that offers a view of the mountains.

To afford the construction of such a home, even after building a home on Jedediah, Harry must have accumulated a fair amount of wealth. His exact business operations are not entirely clear. In the early years, he worked as an insurance agent, as a secretary for City Fuel Co., and then as a mysterious sounding "independent general agent." By early 1900, he had set up a parcel delivery company, Foote's Parcel Express. He met incoming boats and trains and transported goods by horse and cart to their final destination. Family history suggests that Harry organized one of the first mail collection and parcel services in Vancouver. The Vancouver City Directory of 1899 has these entries:

> FOOTE, H.J., agent branch office C.P.R. Telegraph and Dominion Express Co., 341 Carrall, 337 Ninth Ave, Mt. Pleasant, opp. School.

> FOOTE'S PARCEL EXPRESS, 341 Carrall, tel. '378

Harry's office on Carrall was beside what is now known as Pigeon Park but was officially called Pioneer Park, set up on the site of a former rail spur. When Harry's office was there, the electric cars would have been repaired in the BC Electric building the next block over: perhaps it is no surprise that in 1904 he set up an agreement with the BC Electric Railway to deliver goods.

24. A Sojourn Down Under, 1908

While Harry Foote was setting up his businesses, his future son-in-law, Morris Jelly, was travelling first from Jellyby, Ontario to Coast Salish territory—and from there all the way to Sydney, Australia, by ship.

Morris Jelly, approximately age 16–a few years before his trip to Australia.

I wonder if Morris was aware of how privileged he was to be able to travel as he did. Around the time that Morris left his hometown, a "pass system" in Canada required Indigenous peoples to ask for permission to leave reserve lands. These passes were signed by a white Indian Agent, a representative of the federal government.

Even amongst those able to board the ship, passengers could have been denied entry to Australia by the laws at the time. In 1902, Australia had passed the Immigration Restriction Act, also known as the "White Australia Policy." The policy allowed immigration officers to, at their own discretion, require a 50-word dictation in any European language chosen by the officer. It was intended primarily to restrict Asian travellers.[180]

For Morris, however, neither the pass system nor immigration policy were a concern: as a white Canadian, the trip itself required very little preparation. As he said in a letter to his brother: "I didn't make up my mind to come until the day before I sailed." Morris booked a ticket on what was called the Red Route Line, named for the red stripes on the funnel of the S.S. Moana.

Union Steamship Ad.

The route travelled from Sydney to Wellington (New Zealand), Suva (Fiji), Honolulu, and then Victoria and Vancouver, BC. The

---

[180] Since the test could be conducted at whim in any language, the only Asian immigrants who succeeded in entering had strong and influential local sponsors. Immigration Restriction Act of 1901 (commonly known as the White Australia Policy), National Archives of Australia. http://www.naa.gov.au/collection/a-z/immigration-restriction-act.aspx.

advertisement depicted here[181] is from the Union Steamship Company, the company Morris sailed with a few years earlier, listing the Moana.

In the records from April 20, 1908, there is an "M. Jelly," listed as 26 years old. He must have slightly exaggerated his youth, as he would have actually been 28 years old at the time. He and six others are listed as "labourers." There was a crew of 109, and 112 passengers.

Morris's letter to his brother back in Canada reads:

Dear Brother

I suppose you know by this time that I have left Canada for Australia. I should have ritten [sic] sooner but I didn't make up my mind to come until the day before I sailed ... I was acquainted with some of the crew, and they advised me to come to Australia as it was a great country and lots of work.

On his way to Sydney, Morris stopped several times along the way:

We stopped a short time at Honolula, [sic] an American Port. They are all colored peoples long curly hair and very treatcherous [sic] they grow bananas oranges and cocoa nuts there.

His description of Hawaiians as "treatcherous" most likely reflects a cultural stereotype of the time, as this was his first and only visit to the Hawaiian Islands. After his brief stop in Honolulu, Morris landed in Australia on April 20, 1908. Australia wasn't all that he expected, and he was soon disappointed:

---

[181] 1913-14 Union Steam Ship Co. of New Zealand sailing Sydney to San Francisco. Image from http://www.timetableimages.com/maritime/images/union.htm.

> Sydney is the largest city here, population 500,000. It is the most poverty-stricken place I have ever seen. They think more of [$1] here than you would of $10.00 in Canada, living is cheap here, bed and breakfast for .20 cts. They use English money here. This climate is fine. Many people sleep in the parks at night.

His journey to a faraway land wasn't all he had made it out to be before setting off.

> In reguards [sic] to work. Why money wouldn't buy a job here, I have tried everything ...

> I intended to come here for a while and make enough to take me back but there is not chance ... Wages are very low here and even though I did get work it would take me a year to save enough to take me back.

Morris ended his letter by saying:

> If I get back to Canada I will know enough to stay there.

Morris did manage to get enough money to get his passage back to Vancouver—$80 or $90 is what he needed, and perhaps his brother was able to send it over.

And so, just two months later, in June 1908, the Manuka records a 3rd class passenger M. Jelly. It turns out that quite a diverse group were making the journey from Australia to Canada in 1908; Morris describes himself as being the "only Canadian" on board. The composition of the passenger list gives a glimpse into society at the time. There are just two first-class passengers, both British. Then there are 12 people listed as "Chinese," with "ret'd Canadian" under "place of birth." All had left Canada in October or December 1907. Like Morris, it's likely that these Chinese residents of Canada had also made a short sojourn to Australia in search of work. There were 23 people registered as "Japanese"; about half of those were listed as "detained" (without further explanation), and a section of Hanidoos [Hindus] from Honolulu, listed as "deported by U.S. Officials on account of 'trachoma' disease."[182]

And so Morris Jelly returned, along with a group of refugees and returnees, to Canada—and as he had promised in his letter, he stayed in Canada for the rest of his life.

I've come to realize that Morris and I have a fair amount in common: he went to Australia at the age of 28; I went to Nigeria at 23. We both wrote long letters home; his was four pages, my emails were at least that. Both he and I managed to spend all our remaining funds in faraway lands and relied on family or meagre savings to support our passage back.

We were both young white folks with the freedom and ability to travel. We both found benefit from our white skin in our travels. Neither of us, from any records that last, suffered assumptions or lack of opportunities due to our skin colour or ethnic background. We are both part of a culture and social system that, even a hundred years later, allows us to describe other lands and places from a place of friendly, rather distant neutrality. Linda Tuhiwai Smith, a Māori scholar from Aotearoa (New Zealand), writes about the ways white people describe and document the worlds of others. She talks about

---

[182] The note on their destination says Vancouver. Trachoma is a highly infectious eye disease; it was one of the illnesses that resulted in mandatory exclusion by the US immigration department; http://journalofethics.ama-assn.org/2008/04/mhst1-0804.html.

what she calls the "imperial gaze"—a perspective that, whether or not we acknowledge it, both Morris and I have.

25. 1909: Winnie and Morris of Mt. Pleasant

In the fall of 1909, Harry and Mary Ann Foote's middle daughter, Winnie, was 23 years old. She was spending significant time on Jedediah Island. This photo, from around that era, gives a sense of her playful spirit.

Winnie on Jedediah Island.

Her older sister, Olive, had been married at 19 years old; her younger sister Myrtle was engaged to James King, with plans to marry in May 1910.

In this close-up of a photo taken at the Alberta Street house around 1910, 23-year-old Winnie is sitting on the edge of the veranda, slightly separated from the rest. Perched as she is, her feet don't quite reach the floor. Her shoes, shiny dark leather boots with a heel, rest against the porch wall. Her hands are clasped in her lap, fingers interlocked and facing inward. A petticoat peeks out from the end of her long, dark skirt. Her long-sleeved, lacy blouse is high-necked, adorned by a small, dark pendant. She and her younger sister Myrtle are wearing light blouses, in contrast to the stiff, dark formality of their older sister's heavy dress. Seated closest to her father, her face displays the same soft openness as his and yet she seems somehow uncertain, unsure of herself—or maybe of the photographer.

Somehow, that year, she came to meet one Morris Jelly, grandson of Simon Jelly, of Jellyby. When he met Winnie, Jelly was a mature 29 and would have had stories to tell of his recent exploits in Australia.

Perhaps that's part of what he and Winnie got to talking about, we'll never know. By the spring of 1910, a few months before her sister's wedding, Winnie and Morris were planning a "shotgun" wedding.

They married at her parents' home on Broadway, as documented in the local papers of the time. Their first daughter, Thelma, was born five months later, in August 1910.

Thus Winnie Foote married a Jelly, resulting in one rather comical potential hyphenation: the "Foote-Jellys." Fortunately, hyphenation was not yet in vogue and the Jelly name stuck on its own, leaving their descendants to deal with generations' worth of puns and curious questions about spelling. .

Through their marriage, Morris became a part of the Foote family and Foote businesses. Within a few years, he was in business with his brother-in-law, Cecil Foote, at the Main Transfer Co. and then later as Jelly's Express and Baggage Transfer. They put regular advertisements into the Western Call paper,[183] with the catchphrase "Always in Mt. Pleasant."

Phone Fairmont 845 Always in Mt. Pleasant

Jelly's Express and Baggage Transfer

Stand---Main and Broadway

Phone ~ Fairmont 845

Local and Otherwise

Residents on Thirteenth avenue, between Main and Prince Edward streets, would be glad to see the road watered frequently.

Mr. Jelly, who has been handling Jelly's Express, has sold out to Mr. A. F. McTavish, who has been in charge of the livery. Mr. McTavish will now run both the livery and express.

Advertisement for Jelly's Express in Western Call, March 25, 1910

Morris Jelly and Cecil Foote were featured as "businessmen of note" in the August 23, 1912, edition of the Western Call:

---

[183] Quotes and images taken from archive at https://open.library.ubc.ca/collections/bcnewspapers/xwestcall.

> Main Transfer Company
>
> The proprietors of this firm are Messrs. Morris Jelly and S.C. Foote. They are located at 2420 Scotia Street, near the corner of Broadway and Westminster Road ... They are well equipped, and though new in this location are gradually building up a good business. In the transfer service they cater specially for Mt. Pleasant trade. They are anxious to faithfully serve the people of this section of the city.
>
> Again we are impressed with the large number of enterprising young men who are entering into business in Vancouver.
>
> Mr. Jelly is 32 years of age. He was born at Shelburne, Ont. of Canadian parentage. He was raised on the farm, but about fifteen years ago went to Winnipeg and served as a street car conductor. Finally, after a trip to Australia, he decided to settle here, and has now been in Vancouver five years. During this time he has been in the transfer business.
>
> Mr. Foote has seen but 30 years. The place of his nativity was Portage La Prairie. He has resided in this city twenty-one years, and has been engaged with his father for ten years in collection of the mails.
>
> These gentlemen are agreeable and obliging, and are an asset to our growing community.

By all accounts, Morris and Cecil worked hard and were well-liked. There's no doubt that Morris and Cecil had, by luck of birth, benefitted from their European ancestry. At the time, Japanese, Chinese, Indian, and Indigenous men and women were excluded from positions of prestige or public trust; and while this wasn't necessarily something that Morris or Cecil directly supported, it was good news for their growing business. Racist exclusionary policies meant there were fewer businesspeople from Japanese, Chinese, Indian, or Indigenous backgrounds. In businesses like delivery that depended in part on customers' trust, white proprietors were much more likely to be seen as "reliable."

However, it is likely that to Morris and Cecil, this advantage was at best hidden, more likely invisible. It's particularly hard to see the hidden biases in society, both then and now.[184] One hundred years after Cecil and Morris's business, some things haven't changed.

---

[184] Several years ago, researchers in Vancouver and Toronto sent out fake resumes in response to job openings and found that people with Anglo-Saxon-sounding names were 40 percent more likely to receive call-backs for interviews than those with South Asian or Chinese-sounding names—even if the resumes demonstrated the same Canadian education and work experience. Jiménez, Marina (2009). "Right résumé, wrong name"; https://www.theglobeandmail.com/life/right-resume-wrong-name/article4274218/.

26. Jedediah Tragedies: Life and Death in the 1910s

At last, it's time to return to Harry and Mary Ann's homestead on beautiful Jedediah.

In the 1910s, Harry and Mary Ann and their grown children made frequent trips back and forth across the Salish Sea from Vancouver to Jedediah.

The families who spent the most time there, besides Harry and Mary Ann, were those of daughters Winnie Jelly and Olive Olmstead.

In 1912, soon after the Alberta Street house was complete, Olive died in childbirth. Her husband Oscar and three children continued to spend significant time with Harry and Mary Ann on Jedediah.

The Footes, Jellys, and Olmsteads were often joined by cousins and friends. In fact, so many visitors came during the summers that they erected a large tent on a platform next to the house to accommodate the extra guests. Presumably leaning on his contacts in the mail service, Harry arranged mail service to Jedediah Island, and the large wharf in front of the homestead was government-built.[185]

The newlyweds Winnie and Morris spent many of their early years with their first daughter, Thelma, on Jedediah. They visited the island frequently in summer, travelling on the Mary. It was on one of these visits, in early July, that their second child, eight-month-old Mervin Jelly, contracted a bad fever. The nearest hospital was at least several

---

[185] Eileen Bentley, *Jedidiah and Beyond: a Personal History.*

hours away in Pender Harbour, accessible only by boat. Mervin died at that hospital, having not yet reached his first birthday.

In the following autumn, Winnie and Morris conceived their third child: Gordon Jelly. Gordon was born June 1915 in Vancouver, and it seems Winnie and Morris moved to live on Jedediah year-round soon after that.

One motivation for fleeing the city may have been to avoid the Great War recruitment efforts, which eventually became conscription in 1917. Lister Foote, Winnie's youngest brother, just 20 years old when the war broke out, may have joined them on the island for the same reason.

The next year, in the summer of 1916, Lister had an accident. As a Lasqueti author tells the story:

> A son in his teens was out attending to sheep in the hills when he accidentally shot himself. In desperation, he tied his bloody handkerchief to his dog's collar and sent him home. The faithful animal led his family back to him and they tenderly carried him to a waiting boat. They started for Nanaimo, but it was all in vain; he died before they could reach medical aid.[186]

It must have been an incredible loss to have Winnie's brother, Harry and Mary Ann's youngest son, die so suddenly. On Jedediah, he evaded one potential danger only to perish by gunfire close to home.

Again, the family recovered from the tragedy on Jedediah, developing the fields, gardens, and orchards that persist to this day.

---

[186] Muson, Elda Copley. *Lasqueti Island History & Memory*. AdMan Printing 1976.

In the winter of early 1918, Mary Jelly, Winnie and Morris's second daughter, was born in Vancouver. That summer, Winnie and Morris had three children to care for: Thelma, eight years old; Gordon, a toddler of three years; and Mary, just six months old.

In the early 1900s, most adults and children did not know how to swim.[187] As recalled by a neighbour:

> *I especially remember the Foots, Jelleys, and Olmsteads [sic] from Jedediah Island who regularly came with their pots, pans and buckets [to pick blackberries and wild strawberries]. One summer evening we sat watching them loading their pickings, picnic baskets and children into their boats for their return journey. The tide was full and a log running out from the shore was being used as a natural pier from which to embark. There was much running to and fro on the log and the sounds of laughter and banter carried across the water. Suddenly I saw a queer thing; a brown piece of seaweed seemed to be rising and falling in the water near the log.*
>
> *Daddy, what is that? I asked.*
>
> *Instantly he sprang down the slope, ran along the log and pulled out a half-drowned boy. A terrible tragedy had been averted.*[188]

In another anecdote, Thelma, the oldest daughter, was throwing rocks off a cliff and fell into the water. Winnie, unable to swim herself, put her own life in danger to rescue her. Fortunately, both Thelma and Winnie survived this incident.[189] Raising multiple families of

---

[187] it was not until 1946 that the Canadian Red Cross began offering a recognized swimming lesson program.
[188] Muson, Elda Copley. *Lasqueti Island History & Memory*. AdMan Printing 1976.
[189] Eileen Bentley, *Jedidiah and Beyond: A Personal History*.

children in close proximity to the ocean and cliffs must have been particularly challenging, as there would have been no guardrails to hold back young children or toddlers.

Gordon, though born in Vancouver, seems to have spent much of his early years as a baby and toddler on Jedediah. There is record of his name at the island's highest peak, Gibraltar, with his older sister Thelma, when he was just two years old.

On July 27, 1918, in the summer when Thelma was eight, and just after his third birthday, Gordon drowned at Jedediah Island. The exact circumstances of his death are not known.

This last death seems to have been the final straw for the Footes and Jellys. After 1918, the families moved permanently back to Vancouver, and in 1920, they sold Jedediah Island to Henry Hughes of England.

My grandfather, Roy Jelly, was born in 1921, after the Jedediah years. He would have known of Jedediah Island from his sisters and mother, but he didn't talk about the island to his daughters. His elder sister, Thelma, would have remembered those who died on Jedediah Island. She lived much of her life on the coast, before moving to the deserts of Osoyoos, BC. She was an avid hiker and became a strong swimmer: for her 80th birthday, she swam across Osoyoos Lake. I can't help but wonder if she thought of her missing younger brothers as she swam.

As if this wasn't enough trouble for one family, in 1925, Morris Jelly died of influenza and pleurisy, leaving Winnie a widow. By the age of 37, Winnie had lost her youngest brother, two sons, and her husband.

Life was definitely not easy for the Foote family as they faced challenges and struggles. However tragic their losses, there were many others in BC who didn't have the choices they had. Indigenous communities didn't have the luxury of choosing between multiple homes or residences, or even considering "correspondence" school for their children, as the Footes had done on Jedediah. While I cannot in any way undo the ways that my family and I have benefited from our place in colonial society, I can begin to listen for and understand the intergenerational impact of trauma and tragedy - while also acknowledging the many privileges that my ancestors benefited from.

27. The Ancestor I Hope to Be – and an Invitation

In the days, months and years compiling this book, I came to appreciate the ways that colonization is personal, a part of me and of my family, both past and present. Colonization is interwoven into the fabric of my and my family's presence on Turtle Island, past and present.

The process of understanding my own ancestry in relationship to place is a never-ending journey. In the process of this research, I uncovered many more questions than I started with: some of which I may never have a chance to answer. This book captures one portion of a journey that has and I'm sure will continue to transform my thinking, identity, and perspective.

Since beginning this project I have recognized the significant vulnerability inherent in exploring and sharing my own ancestry. In preparing this book, I have revisited this text many times, surprised again and again to uncover assumptions made visible in my chosen words, sources, and adjectives. As Mi'kmaq author Marie Battiste puts it, I am completely and utterly "marinated" in colonization. I'm a fish in water, a colonizer in colonization, a "Canadian" settler on Coast Salish territory.

This project started because I wanted to read someone else's attempt at a family history in connection to colonization in Canada, and I couldn't find one. And so I took the project on myself: I went back through hundreds of years of history to understand my ancestors' stories on Turtle Island and the connections between place, possession, and people. I explored stories from Brita and Rambo in New Sweden in the 1600s, to William Bain on Epekwitk (PEI) in the 1830s, to Harry and Mary Ann Foote on Coast Salish territory in the 1890s.

I look forward to reading your version – and to the conversations I hope will be sparked by these stories.

Epilogue: The Families

In this narrative I've traced the history of my ancestors' families up to the mid-1920s: here are a few tidbits of what came next.

After the Jedediah years, Harry Foote moved into real estate, with offices at 2317 Main Street. By the mid-1920s, he had partnered with former Vancouver mayor Walter Owen. He continued the business until he died in 1937.

After the death of Morris Jelly, my maternal great-grandmother Winnie Foote became a seamstress and milliner, living on her own with her three children. Eventually she remarried to William Davis; when he also died young, she moved back into the Alberta Street home, which she ran as a boarding house. After her mother's death in 1953, Winnie sold the house to an Eastern European family whose son, described earlier, still owned the home as of 2017. Winnie married a third and final time, to Bill Simpson, with whom she moved to Victoria, and lived there until her death in 1962.

After Jedediah Island was sold to Henry Hughes of England, it was owned by several absentee landlords until it was purchased by Al and Mary Palmer of Seattle. Starting in the 1970s, they moved to Jedediah year-round with their three children, living in the original homestead built by the Foote family. Mary Palmer's life and adventures on Jedediah are shared in her 1998 book Jedediah Days. In the early 1990s, as she was preparing to leave the Island, Mary worked with the government of British Columbia and many supporters to have the island designated a park. Jedediah Island Marine Provincial Park is now a protected area and is a popular destination for boaters.

Will Bain, my paternal great-grandfather, lived in Fort Langley until his death in 1962. Ian Bain, his only child, became a professional geologist, studying at the University of Alberta, McGill, and University of Toronto. Ian met his future wife, Claudia Ada Barker—descendent of Peter Rambo, Brita Mattsdotter, and Daniel Springer—in a French language class at McGill University in Montreal. Ian and Claudia's lives are captured in Claudia's 2006 book, Lilies of My Field.

Mabel and Nell Bain lived the rest of their lives in their home and garden in Fort Langley. My father recalled visiting them in the 1960s in Fort Langley, where they continued painting and gardening well into their eighties.

Related Reading

Bain, C.A. (2006). *Lilies of my field.* Vancouver: C.A. Bain.

Barman, J. (2005). *Stanley Park's secret: the forgotten families of Whoi Whoi, Kanaka Ranch and Brockton Point.* Madeira Park, B.C: Harbour Publishing.

Freeman, V. (2000). *Distant Relations: How My Ancestors Colonized North America.* Steerforth Press.

Furniss, E.M., & Cariboo Tribal Council. (1995). *Victims of Benevolence: The Dark Legacy of the Williams Lake Residential School.* Vancouver: Arsenal Pulp Press.

Palmer, M. (1998). *Jedediah days: one woman's island paradise.* Madeira Park, B.C: Harbour Publishing.

Smith, Linda Tuhiwai. (1999). *Decolonizing Methodologies.* Zed Books.

Stó:lō Heritage Trust. (2001). *A Stó:lō-Coast Salish Historical Atlas.* (K. T. Carlson, Ed.). Vancouver: Douglas & McIntyre.

 Mali Bain is a former high school teacher with a background working in university, non-profit, and philanthropic settings. She grew up in Port McNeill on Kwakwaka'wakw territory, northern Vancouver Island; she currently lives, works, and plays on Snuneymuxw territory. She holds degrees in International Relations (B.A.), Education (B.Ed.), and Adult Learning and Education (M.A.). Her master's thesis explored the relationship between an Indigenous family services organization and a UBC department, identifying core principles for relationship-building. What began as a short chapter on "where I come from" ended up being a 5-year journey to extensively research her own family history and connections to colonization in Canada. She supports families to capture their family history in print through NextGen Story: Custom Publishing.

www.ingramcontent.com/pod-product-compliance
Lightning Source LLC
Chambersburg PA
CBHW071418160426
43195CB00013B/1738